GOOD ◆ OLD ◆ DAYS®

Live It Again™

1957

JOHN FALTER

Dear Friends,

Bask in the warmth of your childhood memories when life was carefree, and each day was a new adventure. When friends or siblings were unavailable for playtime, we had that wonderful device, the television, to amuse us. We tuned in to the *Howdy Doody* show and shouted, "It's *Howdy Doody* time!" when prompted by the host. We sang along with the *Mickey Mouse Club* theme song, "Who's the leader of the club that's made for you and me? M-I-C, K-E-Y, M-O-U-S-E!"

When friends or siblings were unavailable for playtime, we had that wonderful device, the television, to amuse us.

Televised Western shows such as *Gunsmoke* and *The Life and Legend of Wyatt Earp* stimulated our imaginations. We put on our cowboy hats, took up our toy pistols and joined the action amid the recorded sounds of pounding horse hooves and gunshots. As adults we were just as enthralled by the action adventures, anticipating each new saga as the story lines unwound.

Dr. Seuss wrote and illustrated a book titled *The Cat in the Hat* that made for fun reading material. We were captivated by the fanciful illustrations and whimsical text. When the daily newspaper arrived at our doors each day, we turned to the comics to laugh along with the escapades of good ol' Charlie Brown and the rest of the *Peanuts* gang, products of the fertile imagination of Charles Schulz. Read more about these famous authors on pages 46 and 47.

Rock 'n' roll continued to be the nation's favorite style of music. Elvis Presley's record sales were boosted into an all-time high with such hits as "All Shook Up" and "Jailhouse Rock." He performed from coast to coast to large audiences. Were you one of those fortunate enough to have seen him live in concert?

Enjoy your walk down memory lane as you browse through pages filled with vintage cars, fabulous fashions and unforgettable celebrities such as New York Yankee catcher Yogi Berra, featured on our cover. Also sprinkled throughout are a medley of memories of daily life in 1957.

Contents

REPRINTED WITH PERMISSION FROM GENERAL MOTORS CO.

REPRINTED WITH PERMISSION FROM SEARS BRANDS, LLC

1957 Quiz

1. Which TV show starred James Arness as Marshal Matt Dillon?
2. What was the 1957 fashion term for capri-type slacks?
3. Who was the first African-American female to win at Wimbledon?
4. What anniversary did the *Howdy Doody* TV show celebrate in 1957?
5. What famous bridge was completed in 1957?
6. What was Dr. Seuss' given name?
7. What baseball team won the 1957 World Series?
8. Who won an Oscar for Best Actor for his role in *The Bridge on the River Kwai*?

Answers are found in this book and on page 127.

957 SEPS

Television Shows for Youngsters

Captain Kangaroo
Fury
Howdy Doody
The Gumby Show
Lassie
Leave It to Beaver
The Mickey Mouse Club
Paul Winchell and Jerry Mahoney
Romper Room
Ruff and Reddy
Disneyland
The Woody Woodpecker Show

Growing Up in 1957

TV for kids

By 1957, children's television programs were a well-established part of the network TV lineup. *Disneyland* was one of the most enduring prime-time series. The show was a masterful blend of cartoons, nature stories and live-action adventure. *Leave It to Beaver* was on TV from 1957 to 1963. The show was a family comedy that centered on life from the perspective of a young boy, Theodore "Beaver" Cleaver. Do you recall the phrase, "Say, kids! What time is it?" The correct answer was, "It's *Howdy Doody* time!" The daytime show attracted millions of baby boomers to the TV set.

In 1957, the *Howdy Doody* show celebrated its 10th anniversary. The show aired from 1947 to 1960. At left is actor Buffalo Bob Smith with his marionette Howdy Doody, and Lew Anderson as Clarabell the Clown. A distinctive aspect of the show was the Peanut Gallery, an onstage bleacher section that held about 40 children.

The Mickey Mouse Club aired daily from 1955 to 1959. Walt Disney spent about $1.125 million on this children's variety show that featured a group of talented kids known as the Mouseketeers. Shown above from left to right in cowboy attire are Mouseketeers Bobby Burgess, Doreen Tracey, Darlene Gillespie, Annette Funicello and Jimmy Dodd.

TV Star Quiz

Match the name of the child celebrity from 1957 with his or her role and TV show.

1. Annette Funicello
2. Jon Provost
3. Angela Cartwright
4. Lauren Chapin
5. Ken Osmond
6. Bobby Diamond

A. Timmy of *Lassie*
B. Kathy Anderson (Kitten) of *Father Knows Best*
C. Joey Newton of *Fury*
D. Mousketeer of *The Mickey Mouse Club*
E. Linda Williams of *The Danny Thomas Show*
F. Eddie Haskell of *Leave It to Beaver*

Answers: 1-D; 2-A; 3-E; 4-B; 5-F; 6-C

The Cleaver family of *Leave It to Beaver* included, clockwise from left, Tony Dow as Wally, Hugh Beaumont as Ward, Jerry Mathers as Beaver and Barbara Billingsley as June.

A magical wonderland of exciting new toys filled the pages of the 1957 Montgomery Ward Christmas catalog. The Blinky Bear at far left was a cushion-soft perfect bedtime toy that sold for $5.98. The electronic Dancing Dan cost $6.49, and the drum was $1.85.

1957 Trivia

Q. What was the name of Roy Rogers' horse?

A. Trigger

This TV storyteller played records synchronized with a picture so the voices seemed to come from the Disney characters on the screen. The toy cost $13.49 and a set of records with filmstrips were $1.98 for a set of five.

Make-believe was more fun when you could dress for the part. The majorette outfit complete with dress, belt, hat, boot-tops and wood baton sold for $4.59. The skater's outfit, perfect for future stars of the ice rink, cost $5.79.

1957 MONTGOMERY WARD

Growing Up in 1957

Playtime fun

Relive the excitement of the treasured toys of 1957, toys that sparked creativity in children. In the days before folks shopped at the local mall, we eagerly awaited the arrival of the toy catalog. Those exciting pages full of dolls, games and novelties were the stuff of dreams. We read every detail of the descriptions, dropping obvious and frequent hints about our top choices to our parents.

1957 MONTGOMERY WARD

This baby in a basket with satin pillow and trim cost $7.98. The doll drank, wet and came with a nursing bottle. When squeezed, big tears rolled down her cheeks.

1957 MONTGOMERY WARD

Stuffed toys were cuddly companions. The French poodle had a curly coat and yipped when her tail was squeezed. The price was $2.98. Zip was a real chimpanzee on the *Howdy Doody* TV show. The stuffed version shown here had a squeaker in one arm and sold for $5.95–8.47, depending on the size ordered.

These dolls came with clothes and a carrying case. The 15-inch bride shown below could walk. The set cost $7.98. The doll at right was 25 inches tall. The set cost $16.49.

1957 MONTGOMERY WARD

1957 MONTGOMERY WARD

Growing Up in 1957

More playtime fun

1957 MONTGOMERY WARD

1957 MONTGOMERY WARD

The 26-inch American-made bike at left was a deluxe model with foot-pedal brakes that sold for $59.95. The English Hercules Tourist bike with matching bag shown above had headlights and taillights, and sold for $47.95.

Kids loved to play make-believe and Western wear was especially popular. The Western rancher outfit above cost $4.79 and was ideal for pretend roundups. The girl's version of Western wear for backyard rodeos was $4.49.

1957 MONTGOMERY WARD

Live-action toys were rugged models of real heavy-duty equipment and cost from $2.59 to $6.98. The toys, made of heavy-gauge steel, all had parts that moved realistically.

Exciting dart games tested both skill and coordination, and included guns that shot the darts. The Mother Hen game at right was $2.69. The Whiz-Bang revolving target below was priced at $1.69.

1957 MONTGOMERY WARD

The Wyatt Earp double holster set for little buckaroos, right, was $5.49. The pistol sold separately for 89 cents. The toys were inspired by the *Wyatt Earp* TV show.

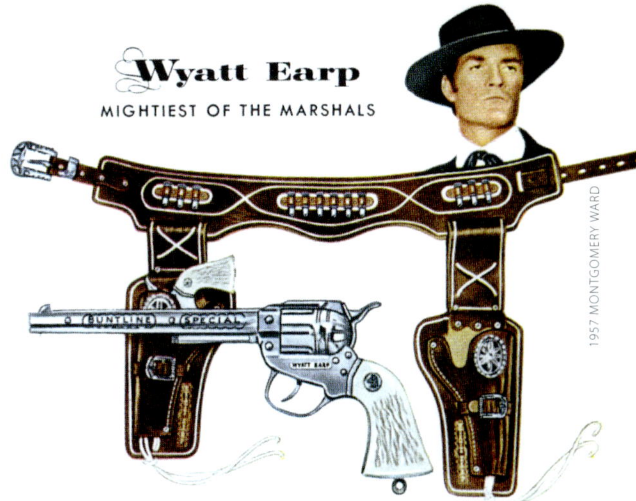

1957 MONTGOMERY WARD

1957 MONTGOMERY WARD

This Career board game cost $2.67. Jump over a mountain … buy a yacht … find uranium. Anything was possible with this exciting new game.

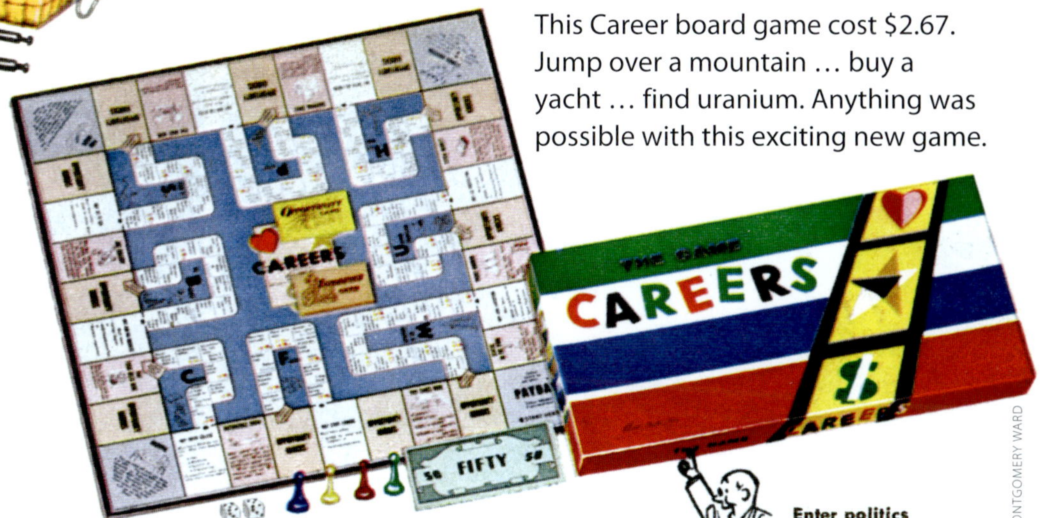

1957 MONTGOMERY WARD

MONTGOMERY WARD

The plastic Zippees, shown at left, buckled onto shoes and were safe, strong and quiet. They were geared for beginners, ages 2–6. The roller skates, ice skates and snow sliders all sold for $2.65.

Growing Up in 1957

Girls' fashions

Little girls of 1957 had the best of both ends of the fashion spectrum. There were charming, full-skirted dresses complemented by matching hats, gloves and anklets. Mothers enjoyed dressing up their little girls for church and parties, and the girls enjoyed looking special too. There was also an assortment of playwear to choose from that was made of cotton and treated so it wouldn't shrink over one percent.

Shimmering party dresses for little girls were washable and priced from $3.77 to $7.74 each. Slips made of yards of tulle were worn underneath to create the billowy look.

Shiny patent-leather shoes made a girl feel like a princess. The shoe stores of 1957 were staffed by friendly clerks who patiently carried shoes back-and-forth from the storeroom to perfectly fit growing feet.

FAMOUS BIRTHDAYS

Katie Couric, January 7 talk-show host, journalist

Mike Bossy, January 22 hockey player (New York Islanders)

Sporty girls enjoyed looking fashionable too, with matching play clothes. The two-piece outfit, above right, came with sunglasses and belt, and cost $2.83. The black pedal pushers were $3.37; blue boxer shorts cost $2.84.

Stylish girls loved a wardrobe of flower-pretty dresses in sizes 7–14. With bows and lace trim, these dresses cost from $4.94 to $7.70.

Coordinated outfits were perfect for springtime and Easter. The six-piece ensemble on the left included a skirt, matching jacket, blouse, petticoat, beret and tote bag for $8.71. The pink pleated skirt and fleecy jacket in the center cost $6.77. The seven-piece outfit at right included gloves, hat and tote bag, priced at $11.74.

These low-priced sport suits were priced from $5.50 to $6.50.

The dress-up set for toddlers, left, came with a shirt with shoulder loops for suspenders, slacks and a belt for $3.98. The gift-boxed set for young boys on the right was $4.98.

The two-piece playsuits, left, sold for about $3. The swimsuit with matching jacket, center, was a fashionable outfit for the beach or pool.

This Roy Rogers knit shirt with fringe was $1.37.

Growing Up in 1957

Boys' attire

For dress-up occasions, little boys were carbon copies of their fathers, wearing handsome sport suits paired with dress shirts and ties. Most playwear was made of comfortable, washable, durable cotton. Suspenders helped keep the pants in place for active toddlers. Sweaters were made of extra-heavy, warm and long-wearing Orlon that was quick-drying and shrink-resistant.

1957 Trivia

Q. What fictitious city did the Cleaver family call home in the TV show *Leave It to Beaver?*

A. Mayfield

Popular crew-neck knit shirts were priced at $1.20 each.

Fraternity prep jackets in boys' sizes 8–18 cost from $6.70 to $6.99.

Ski-style sweaters were perfect for the cold days of winter and sold for $3.98 to $4.98, depending on the size ordered.

Growing Up in 1957

Child's play

Playtime was the essence of childhood. In those bygone days we were bursting with vim and vigor, looking for ways to pack our lives with fun. Most of us were up with the sun each day and didn't run out of energy until our heads hit the pillow at night.

The highlight of many a boy's summer was that homerun that soared out of the park, amazing or stunning all those who witnessed it, depending on which team you were cheering for.

"Aw, Mom, football players don't wear rubber boots," grumbled the pint-size athlete. But the boy must obey orders or get benched—at home!

Playing dress-up in Mom's clothes was so much fun. Even better was adding lipstick as the finishing touch, though it sure wasn't easy to apply with unpracticed little fingers.

The Metro Daily News

FINAL EDITION

JANUARY 16, 1957

U.S. BUDGET PROPOSAL SURPLUS

President Eisenhower's budget proposal for the upcoming year calls for a $1.8 billion surplus.

Mom insists her offspring dress up and learn to dance, though they don't look eager for the opportunity, especially when other boys who look ready for some all-boy activity mock their entrance into the dance studio.

Simple activities, like linking hands to play ring around the rosie or putting on rubber boots to splash to your heart's content after a heavy rain, are part of the magical memories of childhood.

"It's very generous of you, Russell, but I don't believe your resignation would help our crowded school situation."

When the lunch bell rang, there was a stampede to the cafeteria. Many schools provided healthy hot meals or kids dug into their packed lunches to see what goodies their mothers had included.

Sometimes Mom chauffeured the kids to school, allowing them to sleep later, and sent them off with a smile and a wave.

Eager students make for a happy classroom atmosphere. Every class had at least one student who struggled with speaking out of turn and shouted, "I know, I know, call on me, teacher!"

Not all schools had a library at the elementary level, but the children who did have access to books and a librarian were more eager and excited about learning to read.

School Years

Learning the basics

Life for the kids of 1957 wasn't all fun and games. There were those necessary hours set aside for the required schooling. Most children did not arrive for that very first day of school able to identify the alphabet, numbers or colors. Their initial experiences with learning were more about being taught to take turns, use good manners and organize belongings. It wasn't long, though, until teachers got down to the business of filling young minds with fundamental words and math facts.

FROM THE COLLECTION OF BARB SPRUNGER

Dick and Jane were the main characters of one of the most popular basic readers used by schools. Many children learned to read with this series that included supporting characters such as Spot the dog, Puff the cat and Tim the teddy bear.

FROM THE COLLECTION OF BARB SPRUNGER

©1957 SEPS

No one loses more things than a young boy. The missing mitten, just beyond the boy's reach, made its way to the lost and found, but the necessary boot is nowhere in sight.

© 1957 SEPS

"This report card is not indicative of your maximum potential!"

School Years

Teen scene

There was a variety of fun after-school events for teenagers to choose from. Many boys and girls received allowances to spend on movies, magazines, sodas and hamburgers. In 1957, teen boys ran around in letter jackets and cuffed jeans; girls wore poodle skirts, saddle shoes and bobby socks. It was an idyllic time of going steady, cheerleading, sports, dances and that all-important first date. The high school set frequently met after school at the local soda shop to compare cars, socialize and complain about homework to the background music of a jukebox. It was a time to check out the crowd for possible future dates.

1957 Trivia

Q. Under what name did Paul Simon and Art Garfunkel begin their recording career?

A. Tom and Jerry

For teenagers, few things were quite as stimulating as a soda shop filled with their peers exchanging greetings, wisecracks and laughter. Add ice cream and soft drinks, and the place was the ideal after-school spot to hang out.

Nearly every girl studied the fine art of homemaking during home economics class at school. The proper way to set a table for fine dining was explained and practiced. Simple sewing projects were attempted and completed to the teacher's satisfaction.

FAMOUS BIRTHDAYS

LeVar Burton, February 16 actor (Kunta Kinte of *Roots*)

Vanna White, February 18 game-show host (letter turner of *Wheel of Fortune*)

Baton twirling was a popular extracurricular activity that combined grace and agility, adding flair to marching-band performances. The girls sharpened their skills by attending baton-twirling clinics during the summer.

Brothers are nice to have, especially when they grow up and stop eavesdropping during phone conversations. A girl needs privacy to talk to boys or talk *about* boys with girlfriends.

What Made Us Laugh

"My advice to you is to leave the keys in the ignition and hope somebody steals it."

"I don't feel too selfish—George had all the fun of giving it to me."

"We can do without your opinion, Osborne."

"Bringing up five teenage daughters is no easy job."

"Pribbly, we've been getting complaints about these high-pressure methods of yours."

"There's nothing wrong with her eyes. Her ponytail is too tight."

"It's tough to say goodbye to all this … the campus … these halls of ivy … friends … my allowance …"

"I understand they paid $250,000 for him."

The main cast of *Gunsmoke* was, left to right, James Arness as Marshal Matt Dillon, Dennis Weaver as Chester Goode, Amanda Blake as Kitty Russell and Milburn Stone as Doc Adams.

Actor Richard Boone fires a Colt .45 revolver during a scene from *Have Gun Will Travel*, a Western that ran from 1957 to 1963.

Show host Hal March and contestant Robert Strom of *The $64,000 Question* appeared on the cover of TV Guide. Robert Strom, 10-year-old prodigy, became the winner of one of TV's biggest jackpots, winning a total of $224,000.

Garry Moore reads his lines on his show, *I've Got a Secret*. The original series was seen on television from 1952 to 1967. The format of the show was simple—four panelists took turns questioning the contestants to reveal their secrets.

Our Favorite TV Shows

Television was well-established by 1957. There were an estimated 63 million television sets in the world with about 50 million in the United States alone, where watching television was a top leisure activity. *Gunsmoke* introduced the "adult Western" to TV. The No. 1 show in 1957 was set in Dodge City, Kan., in the 1870s. The series was long-lived, running from 1955 to 1975.

Quiz shows such as *You Bet Your Life*, *I've Got a Secret* and *The $64,000 Question* drew large audiences with prize money reaching new heights. Situation comedies like *December Bride*, starring Spring Byington, and *The Danny Thomas Show* were also popular. These sitcoms used the same basic formula: humor, a problem solved and a lesson learned.

Tops on Television

Gunsmoke
CBS

The Danny Thomas Show
CBS

Tales of Wells Fargo
NBC

Have Gun Will Travel
CBS

I've Got a Secret
CBS

The Life and Legend of Wyatt Earp
ABC

General Electric Theater
CBS

The Restless Gun
NBC

December Bride
CBS

You Bet Your Life
CBS

Handsome Hugh O'Brian starred as Wyatt Earp on *The Life and Legend of Wyatt Earp*. Story lines included themes related to politics and family relationships along with the usual action of Western programs.

You Bet Your Life, a quiz show hosted by Groucho Marx, featured a different cast each week. People watched to see who would appear with Marx and listen to his humorous comments. Marx was television's master of the comic insult. He said, "I'll bet you've never thought about me this way, but I'm probably the only man in America who can offend nobody. I've been insulting so many people on my show for so many years that nobody thinks I mean it anymore!"

Our Favorite TV Shows

Kids say the darndest things!

Art Linkletter's House Party, seen in the afternoons from 1952 to 1970, brought a new type of humor to television—funny, innocent comments by children. The show opened with jokes, quizzes and guest experts, but the highlight for most of the viewers was when Linkletter interviewed children who ranged in age from 5 to 10. Their spontaneous replies to his questions were priceless, often stunning the intrepid host. When asked about his haircut, a 6-year-old boy said he told his barber, "Give me a haircut just like my dad's—with a hole on top!"

"My mother's OK, I guess, except that she runs around the house in her nightgown all day."

Cleanliness is sometimes achieved by desperate methods. Mr. Linkletter remarked to a 6-year-old that she had wonderful teeth. "How do you keep them that way?"

"Oh," she said, "I sneak into my big brother's bathroom and use his big red toothbrush when he's not looking."

© 1957 SEPS

Over nationwide TV, this young lady announced her definition of a grandmother: "A nice, old gray-haired lady who keeps your mommy from spanking you."

"Who can think," Art Linkletter asked, "of some bad table manners to watch out for?"

"Don't put your food in other people's drinks."

"Don't use your dress for a napkin when your mother's looking."

"Don't throw food under the table if there's not a dog under there, because it'll rot."

"You should always turn your head when you sneeze at the table, but you'd better grab your plate and take it with you, because then people can't sneak vegetables on your plate that you don't want while your head's turned."

"Did your father give you any advice on how to behave on television?" the boy was asked. "He just told me one thing," was the reply. "Keep my zipper up."

"I'd like to have a ton of vanishing cream. Then, when my big brother got ready to punch me, I'd put on the cream and vanish."

Art Linkletter asked several children this question: "What did your mommy tell you not to say?" Here are a few of the answers:

"My mother told me not to tell any of the family secrets, like the time she dyed her hair blonde, and it came out purple."

"My mommy said to keep quiet about her condition, but I don't know what a 'condition' is. She just keeps getting fatter and fatter every week."

"My daddy told me not to laugh too loud, and no matter where it itches, don't scratch anywhere."

© 1957 SEPS

Based on the well-known comic strip by Chic Young, *Blondie* episodes were simple and often about Dagwood's conflicts with his boss, Mr. Dithers. Whenever Dagwood was in trouble, he always managed to stumble and bumble his way out of it. As in the comic strip, he loved huge sandwiches and loudly called for his wife, Blondie, at the first sign of trouble.

COURTESY EVERETT COLLECTION

Actor John Forsythe was the main character in *Bachelor Father*. Noreen Corcoran played his niece, who enthusiastically tried to find the perfect wife for her uncle.

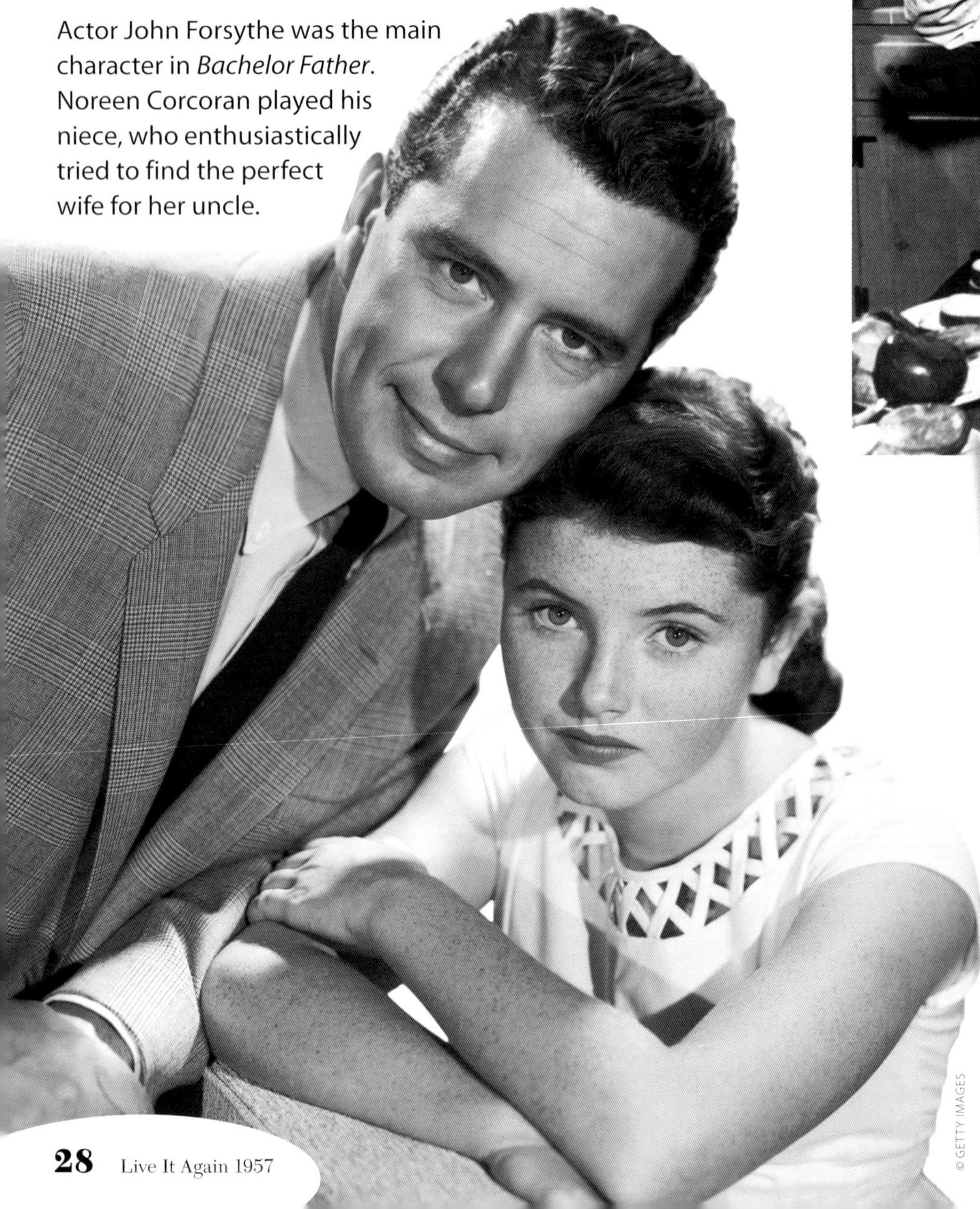

© GETTY IMAGES

Television Shows Debuting in 1957

Bachelor Father
The Billy Graham Crusade
Blondie
Chet Hutley Reporting
The Jimmy Dean Show
Maverick
Perry Mason
Wagon Train
Zorro

Our Favorite TV Shows

1957 debuts

Blondie was a favorite comic strip that was made into a movie in 1938, the first of 28 films. In 1957, NBC brought the story to television with familiar Bumstead family characters: Dagwood, Blondie and their children, Alexander and Cookie. *Bachelor Father* aired from 1957 to 1962 and featured character Bentley Gregg, played by John Forsythe, a Hollywood attorney with many gorgeous women as clients. He was the legal guardian for his niece Kelly, played by Noreen Corcoran. *Maverick* first came to television in 1957 and aired until 1962, starring James Garner as a wisecracking ladies' man. The swashbuckling adventures of *Zorro* ran from 1957 through 1959. *Perry Mason*, starring Raymond Burr, became the most successful lawyer series on television.

The show *Maverick* starred James Garner as cardsharp Bret Maverick. The Western successfully combined humor with a non-stop flow of action adventures.

TV Trivia

Q. In what 1960s TV show did Zorro star Guy Williams play Prof. John Robinson?

A. Lost in Space

Guy Williams played Zorro, a man who presented himself as a passive aristocrat, but on the sly donned a mask and sword to aid the oppressed of Spanish California. He used his sword to slash the letter "Z" at the scenes of his rescue as his calling card.

Owners of this Olympic television that sold for $129.95 enjoyed three types of entertainment from one unit—TV, radio and phonograph—complete with high-fidelity sound.

Home Electronics

TV choices

No other household technology, not even indoor plumbing or the telephone, was as wholeheartedly embraced as the television. It wasn't long until TV was the most important single form of entertainment for people who had once spent their evenings at the movies, reading or listening to the radio. In 1952, televisions were in 17 million homes. By 1957, 41 million homes had a set. Color televisions were available, but they were more expensive and complicated to operate than black-and-white sets. There wasn't a whole lot of color programming available, either, so most Americans were content to stick with their black-and-white models.

No more fiddling with the tuner on this General Electric television. Just push one button for a pre-tuned picture. G.E. cut six inches off the cabinet depth for a new, slim silhouette. A remote control was included at no extra cost.

The portable Philco "Slender Seventeener" was one of the most portable televisions in 1957. It was a big-screen TV in a small, lightweight case that could be taken everywhere. The powerful antenna rotated to locate the strongest signal. This model was available in bright colors as well as wood tones for $159.95.

"Where were you when Cleveland was ahead?"

Only Admiral's remote control worked with this model's radio-phonograph as well as the TV. It turned the unit on and off, controlled the volume and changed TV channels.

1957 ADMIRAL

FAMOUS BIRTHDAYS

Spike Lee, March 20 film director (*Do the Right Thing*)

Leeza Gibbons, March 26 TV personality (host of *Entertainment Tonight*)

Home Electronics

Favorite gadgets

We rejoiced when each new gadget entered the market. It was an exciting time when we were awakened by the music of clock radios and enthralled by the exciting new features included in cameras and phonographs. The fascinating new devices were shrinking in size for greater portability in an era of on-the-go lifestyles.

"I thought we'd never get the camera back from that bear!"

For $34.95, the owner of this clock radio was awakened to soothing music.

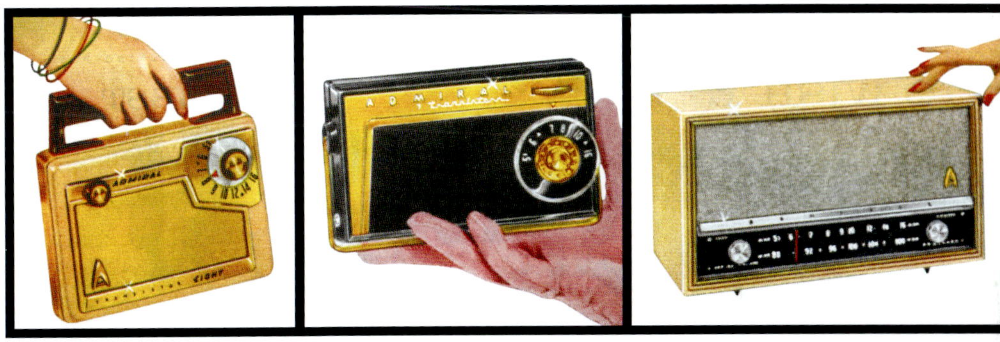

Smaller transistor radios were easy to transport. The Admiral models at left and middle were $29.95 each and could play in trains, planes and cars. The deluxe AM-FM table radio at right was $15.95.

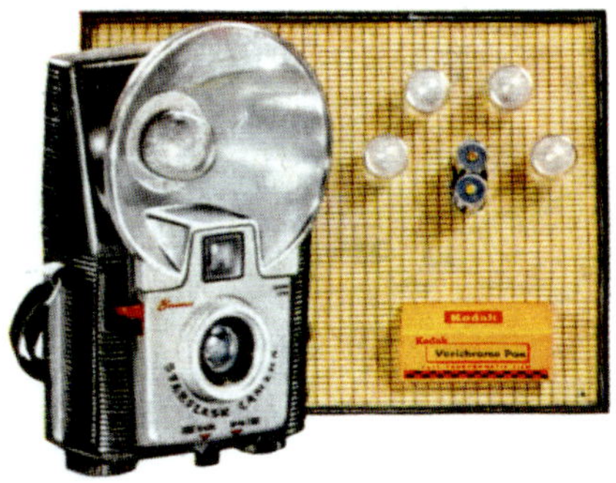

Kodak cameras were available in a variety of models. The 35mm camera, above left, was $58.40. The Brownie Starfish camera above could take snapshots in black-and-white or color, and sold for $9.95. The movie camera at left was $104.70.

Sounds of 1957

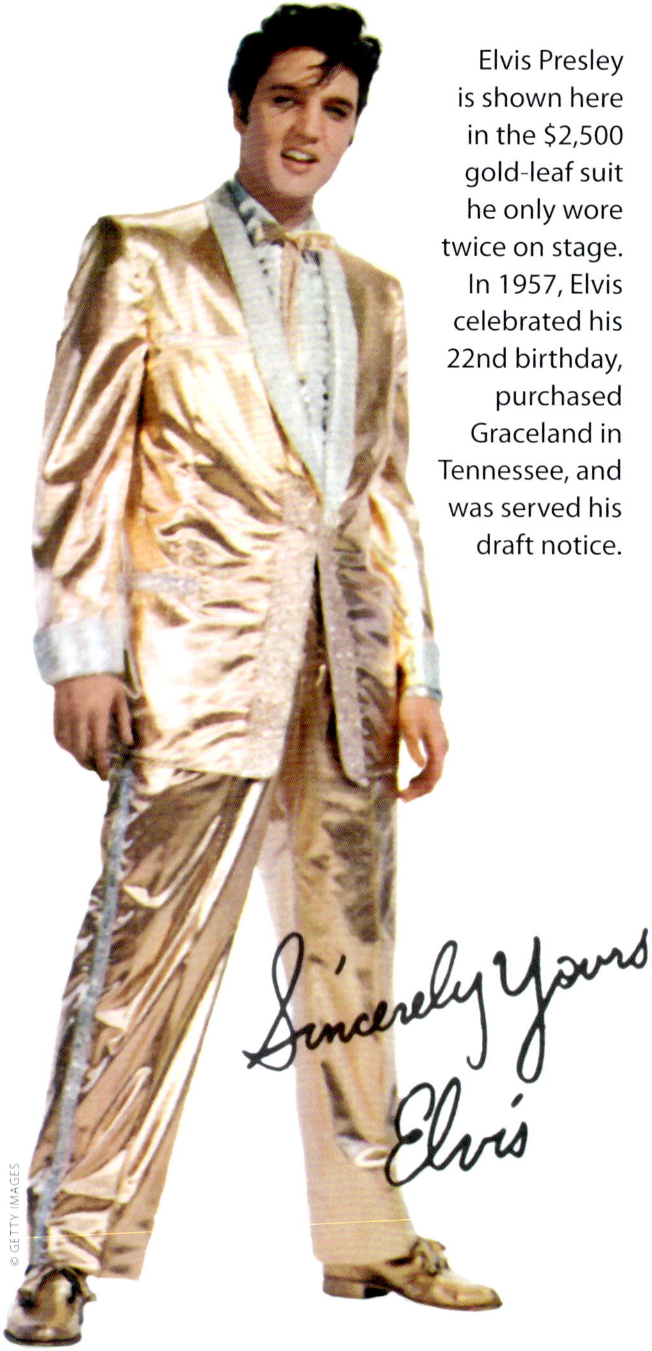

Elvis Presley is shown here in the $2,500 gold-leaf suit he only wore twice on stage. In 1957, Elvis celebrated his 22nd birthday, purchased Graceland in Tennessee, and was served his draft notice.

Elvis Presley had three of the top songs in 1957 along with making two movies, *Loving You* and *Jailhouse Rock*. He continued to perform live and expanded his concerts to Canada and Hawaii, thrilling audiences that included screaming teen girls. Presley made his third and final appearance on the *Ed Sullivan Show*, seen only from the waist up due to censorship of his dance movements. For parents who were worried about the effect of rock 'n' roll on their children, there was Pat Boone. He didn't drink, smoke, curse or dance suggestively, and he was happily married. Debbie Reynolds, known for being perky and energetic, also combined a film career with the top hit song "Tammy."

MEMORABLE QUOTE

"I've always wanted to stay involved with young people. I never bought into the idea that entertainers owe nothing to their audience except a good performance."

—Pat Boone

Singer Pat Boone signing his autograph on concert programs. He was the second most popular singer of 1957 behind Elvis Presley. Boone's trademark was his white bucks, a shoe style that became very fashionable.

Tab Hunter was a handsome actor who starred in over 50 movies and also had success with the record "Young Love." His recording went to No. 1 on the charts, knocking Elvis out of the top position for 12 straight weeks.

Top Hits of 1957

"All Shook Up"
Elvis Presley

"Love Letters in the Sand"
Pat Boone

"Jailhouse Rock"
Elvis Presley

"(Let Me Be Your) Teddy Bear"
Elvis Presley

"April Love"
Pat Boone

"Young Love"
Tab Hunter

"Tammy"
Debbie Reynolds

"Honeycomb"
Jimmie Rodgers

"Wake Up Little Susie"
The Everly Brothers

"You Send Me"
Sam Cooke

In 1957, the movie *Tammy and the Bachelor* gave Debbie Reynolds a No. 1 song on the charts with the sentimental ballad, "Tammy." Reynolds first became a celebrity for her role in the 1952 movie, *Singin' in the Rain*.

American Bandstand first aired on ABC in August of 1957. Dick Clark hosted the TV show where teenagers danced to Top 40 hits. The popular teen record party was shown in the late afternoon just as students were out of school for the day. Clark's clean-cut boy-next-door appearance added to the success of the show.

Music Trivia

Q. What 1957 hit song written and performed by Chuck Berry also became a hit for the Beatles in 1965?

A. "Rock 'n' Roll Music"

Jerry Lee Lewis became popular in 1957 with his string of hits, including "Whole Lotta Shakin' Goin' On," and "Great Balls of Fire." When performing, he would often play the piano standing, sit on the keyboard, or even stand on top of the piano.

Sounds of 1957

Rocking to the beat

Rock 'n' roll was in full swing by 1957. Chuck Berry was known by many as the "father of rock 'n' roll." He was the one individual who rightfully came closest to being credited with introducing the genre as it is known today. In 1957, rock 'n' roll represented two-thirds of the 60 top-selling records in the United States. Rock 'n' roll was performed and also written by young people, and it focused on what was important to them, including slang, love and freedom. Advancements in record technology also had a part in the success of rock 'n' roll. A 45-rpm record sold for as little as 69 cents. Teenagers could stack up 10 of these 7-inch single records on a portable record player and have a dance party.

Chuck Berry brought vitality and spirit to rock 'n' roll. His compositions combined a number of traditional music styles and appealed to a wide variety of audiences. His toe-tapping music and rapid-fire lyrics became the anthems of a generation of teenagers. He had hits in 1957 with "School Days" and "Rock and Roll Music."

Buddy Holly was known as one of the best rock 'n' roll songwriters. In 1957, he wrote and recorded his first hit, "That'll Be the Day," with his group The Crickets. Between August 1957 and August 1958, he had seven hit singles. He was an up-and-coming star when he was killed in a plane crash in 1959 at age 22.

Tops at the Box Office

The Bridge on the River Kwai
Sayonara
Peyton Place
Gunfight at the O.K. Corral
A Farewell to Arms
The Pride and the Passion
Island in the Sun
Jailhouse Rock
Les Girls
I Was a Teenage Werewolf

The Big Screen

The biggest challenge for moviemakers in 1957 was to win back ticket buyers who had turned to television for most of their entertainment. *The Bridge on the River Kwai* was the top box office draw and told the story of a British colonel and prisoner of war, played by Alec Guinness, who cooperated with his Japanese captors to build a railway bridge, not knowing the Allies planned to destroy it. The movie *Sayonara* produced an Oscar for Best Supporting Actor for Red Buttons, and Best Supporting Actress for Miyoshi Umeki as Katsumi. Marlon Brando was the star of the film as Maj. Lloyd "Ace" Gruver and was nominated for Best Actor, but did not win the award. Elvis Presley starred in *Jailhouse Rock*, a movie about a young man serving time for manslaughter, who became a teenage rock star.

The Pride and the Passion was a historic film that dealt with how the Spaniards took their country back from the French who were under the command of Napoleon. The movie starred Italian sex symbol Sophia Loren as Juana, shown at right, Cary Grant as Anthony and Frank Sinatra as Miguel.

Left to right are actors Alec Guiness, William Holden and Jack Hawkins on the set of the movie, *The Bridge on the River Kwai*. The film won several Oscars, including Best Picture, Best Actor for Alec Guiness, Best Director for David Lean and Best Music Scoring for Malcolm Arnold.

Miiko Taka and Marlon Brando star in the film *Sayonara*. In the romance, a United States air force major in Kobe, Japan, falls for a beautiful entertainer and faces his own personal issues with interracial marriage.

© GETTY IMAGES

© GETTY IMAGES

This is one of the posters for the Elvis Presley film *Jailhouse Rock*. The impressive music from the movie included the songs "Jailhouse Rock," "One More Day," "Young and Beautiful," "Don't Leave Me Now" and "I Want to Be Free."

Willie Mays of the New York Giants, one of the best all-around baseball players, is photographed while stretching during spring training.

Actress Jayne Mansfield, a leading sex symbol, enjoyed the spotlight. She made pink her trademark color by driving a pink car and living in a house decorated with pink that she called "the Pink Palace." More people saw her in photographs than in her movies. From just September 1956 to May 1957, Mansfield appeared in approximately 2,500 newspaper photographs.

Performers Bobby Troup, Julie London, Peter Potter, Anna Maria Alberghetti and Robert Clary warm up for a television performance.

Frank Gifford of the New York Giants was professional football's all-around man. He played both receiver and running back; then he made a second career in sports broadcasting for TV and radio.

"It's taken me almost all my 30 years to be an 'overnight success'," said Harry Belafonte, who made millions of dollars with his folk songs. He began a career in acting before becoming a famous musician.

Extraordinary People

The standout people of 1957 featured here range from sports heroes to actors and singers. Celebrities become accustomed to having their photographs taken, whether in the midst of exercising their own particular talents or when in public just going about the business of life.

Clark Gable and Doris Day are photographed on the set of the movie *Teacher's Pet*. Gable represented the American ideal of masculinity for decades. Doris Day became famous through a series of popular film musicals.

MEMORABLE QUOTE

"I'm just a lucky slob from Ohio who happened to be in the right place at the right time."

—Clark Gable

Actor Hugh O'Brian, known for his role on the television show *The Life and Legend of Wyatt Earp*, frolicked with water skier Delores Kipple.

Comedian Phil Silvers and his sidekick, Maurice Gosfield, rehearse for a scene from their television show, *Sergeant Bilko*.

Extraordinary People

Families of the celebrities

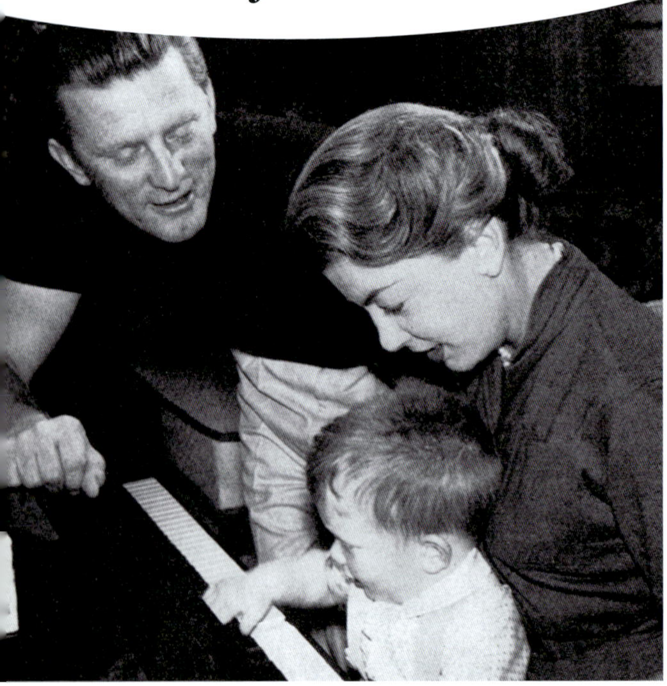

Actor Kirk Douglas is shown with his wife, Anne, and their son, Peter Vincent. Douglas was nominated for Oscars for his roles in the movies *Champion*, *The Bad and the Beautiful* and, in 1957, *Lust for Life*.

Tennessee Ernie Ford, his wife Betty and two boys, Jeffrey and Brion, enjoying family time. The singer and host of the TV variety program, *The Ford Show*, valued his happy home more than fame or money.

Dinah Shore married actor George Montgomery in 1943. They are shown with son Jody and daughter Melissa Ann. Dinah was an award-winning TV personality who won nine Emmys, a Peabody Award and a Golden Globe.

The Metro Daily News

FINAL EDITION

MARCH 26, 1957

ELVIS PRESLEY PURCHASES GRACELAND

Elvis buys home near Memphis, Tenn.

Golfer Jack Burke Jr., PGA Player of the Year in 1956, is pictured with wife Ielene and children Mary Ielene, John Joseph III and Michael. He said, "Somehow, my marriage and my outside interests have allowed my golf game to take its proper place in life."

Actress Eve Arden of the *Our Miss Brooks* TV show is enjoying family time at Christmas.

June Allyson's smoky voice and sunny personality made her a box-office draw. In 1945 she married actor-director Dick Powell. The couple is shown with their son, Ricky, and daughter, Pamela.

Actor Ernest Borgnine, who won an Academy Award as Best Actor for his role in the 1955 film *Marty*, takes his daughter Nancy shopping for Christmas gifts.

With talent, looks and a fortune at their disposal, the Kennedy family became known as "America's Royal Family." Joseph P. Kennedy, center, patriarch of the family, is shown with, from left to right, son Edward, daughters Patricia and Jean, and Jean's husband, Steven Smith.

John Clymer, Featured Cover Artist

Artist John Clymer was born in 1907 in Ellensburg, Wash. Located in the foothills of the Cascade Mountains, the beautiful setting cultivated his love of the outdoors. After graduation, he painted billboards and signs to pay for art school. John knew that most of the work in illustration was on the East Coast, so he moved to Westport, Conn. Between the years of 1942 and 1962, Clymer's artwork graced the pages of *The Saturday Evening Post* with over 80 covers and many story illustrations. His interest in Western landscapes was revived after World War II, when he painted inspiring panoramic views. He died in 1989 in Jackson Hole, Wyo.

MEMORABLE QUOTE

"When I got into my early teens, like all boys, I got to wondering what in the world could I do to make a living and live in the mountains? One day I got to thinking about it and thought, 'That's it! I'll paint pictures, and then I can live wherever I want to live.'"

—John Ford Clymer

The illustrations here and on the facing page are Clymer's 1957 *Saturday Evening Post* covers.

FROM THE COLLECTION OF BARB SPRUNGER

"Look at me!
Look at me now!"
said the cat.
"With a cup and a cake
on the top of my hat!
I can hold up two books!
I can hold up the fish!
And a little toy ship!
And some milk on a dish!
And look!
I can hop
up and down
on the ball!
But that is not all!
Oh, no.
That is not all …"

© 1957 SEPS

Best-Selling Books of 1957

By Love Possessed
by James Gould Cozzens

Peyton Place
by Grace Metalious

Compulsion by Meyer Levin

Rally Round the Flag, Boys!
by Max Shulman

Blue Camellia
by Frances Parkinson Keyes

Eloise in Paris
by Kay Thompson

The Scapegoat
by Daphne du Maurier

On the Beach by Nevil Shute

Below the Salt
by Thomas B. Costain

Atlas Shrugged by Ayn Rand

Theodor Geisel, better known as Dr. Seuss, captured the imagination of children with his fanciful book characters and illustrations. Millions of his books have sold worldwide. He is shown below as he works on drawings for *How the Grinch Stole Christmas*.

© LIBRARY OF CONGRESS, PRINTS AND PHOTOGRAPHS DIVISION, FSA 3C24309U

Cartoons and Novels

"I was born to draw comic strips," said Charles Schulz, the creator of *Peanuts*. He grew up enjoying reading the funnies with his father. After he served in the Army during World War II, he concentrated on his cartoon career. In 1950, Schulz's dream of creating a nationally syndicated daily comic strip came true when *Peanuts* was accepted by United Feature Syndicate. Many came to love the *Peanuts* gang of characters—Charlie Brown, Lucy, Snoopy, Schroeder and Linus. The five cartoons on this page appeared in *The Saturday Evening Post*—the top three in 1957 and the bottom two in 1948.

Dr. Seuss was the pen name of Theodor Seuss Geisel. He was not a medical doctor, but a writer and illustrator of children's books. In the 1950s, people thought there was a literary problem among children caused by boring reading primers, such as the *Dick and Jane* series. A publishing company asked Geisel to create a new primer, resulting in *The Cat in the Hat*, first published in 1957. It was anything but dull.

Charlie Brown, Schulz's baffled little hero, and Snoopy, one of Charlie's critics.

Linus with his cherished blanket. It provided him with comfort, security and an "indescribable happiness."

Schroeder is a musical genius. Lucy's overtures fail to win him from her competitor, Beethoven.

"Good grief, woman, get out of the way! Do you want to be trampled to death?"

"We must be approaching civilization … I can see my mother!"

Cartoonist Charles Schulz, wife Joyce and their four children are shown at left. The main character, Charlie Brown, was based on Schulz's memories of his schoolboy days when he struggled to be a success. As an adult in the 1950s, his drawing skills brought fame and a $50,000-a-year income.

What Made Us Laugh

"Now I'll show you what I meant by its being shockproof."

"It's a father! I'm an 8-pound girl!"

"Wait a minute! You just charged me $1.15 for my own child."

"The glasses are straight, all right—it's your head that's crooked!"

"Sold to the lady in the black hat for thirty-five cents!"

"Cleanest shop in town."

"It's much too tight—I'll take it!"

"No other tonic can make thish shtatement."

President Eisenhower's Second Term Begins

COURTESY NATIONAL PARK SERVICE AND DWIGHT D. EISENHOWER PRESIDENTIAL LIBRARY & MUSEUM 68-349-9

Dwight and Mamie Eisenhower along with son John and his wife Barbara are shown at the inaugural ball.

Eisenhower won by 9.5 million votes in the election of 1956, second only to FDR's record-smashing 11-million vote edge in 1936. Ike's victory garnered the largest vote received by a Republican candidate at the time. Because the official inaugural date of January 20 fell on a Sunday, President Eisenhower took the oath for office in a private White House ceremony. He was formally inaugurated again for the public on Monday, January 21, on the east portico of the White House. In his inaugural address, President Eisenhower indicated his dedication to "the building of a peace with justice in a world where moral law prevails." One of his major victories of the year was Congressional approval of most of his foreign aid recommendations. The year was not without its struggles, however. On November 25, 1957, Eisenhower suffered a mild stroke, but he recovered rapidly.

COURTESY NATIONAL PARK SERVICE AND DWIGHT D. EISENHOWER PRESIDENTIAL LIBRARY & MUSEUM 72-2063-85

President Eisenhower, left, is standing with his grandchildren, Anne and David Eisenhower. Vice President Nixon, right, is standing with daughters Julie and Tricia. David and Julie later become husband and wife. Looking at the photograph, one might think David already had an interest in Julie.

President Eisenhower is holding his weekly press conference. He greatly improved communication with the people of the United States by being more accessible to the media.

© 1957 SEPS

President Eisenhower was sworn in for his second term as President of the United States. In the afternoon, 750,000 spectators watched a 3½-hour parade. The highlight of the parade was a mammoth 408-foot-long float that introduced the theme "Liberty and Strength Through Consent of the Governed."

From left to right, President Eisenhower and Secretary of State John Foster Dulles greeted the visiting South Vietnam President Ngo Dinh Diem at the Washington National Airport in May.

COURTESY OF NATIONAL PARK SERVICE, EISENHOWER NATIONAL HISTORIC SITE

Ike and Mamie Eisenhower enjoy an evening out. Though Mamie did not ever earn a paycheck for work outside the home, she had a full-time job for most of her life. She said, "Ike was my career."

The Edsel, named after Henry Ford's son, was extensively test-marketed and researched. Unfortunately, the car's hype did not match expectations, resulting in low sales and losses for the Ford Motor Co.

Queen Elizabeth and Prince Philip of Great Britain visited the United States in 1957. From left to right before a state dinner at the White House are Queen Elizabeth, President Dwight D. Eisenhower, Mamie Eisenhower and Prince Philip.

Evangelist Billy Graham preaches at Madison Square Garden in New York City, drawing record crowds.

National Headlines

Headliners of 1957 included the coming-out party of Ford Motor Co.'s heavily advertised new car, the Edsel. The car was introduced with much fanfare on Sept. 4, 1957, dubbed "E-Day."

Mother Nature also caused a number of headlines. The landfall of Hurricane Audrey resulted in catastrophic damage across Texas and Louisiana. A powerful F5 tornado wreaked destruction along a 71-mile path across Kansas and into Missouri.

Billy Graham was a forceful young preacher with a basic message—sinners should confess their sins, accept Christ and be saved. He was known for his large revival meetings. In 1957, his New York City crusade filled Madison Square Garden for four months.

During the 1950s, Americans thought warnings about the Mafia and organized crime were unfounded until a police raid uncovered a national meeting of over 100 mafiosi in Apalachin, N.Y. Many were arrested, creating a field day for law enforcement and journalists.

U.S. News

The Rev. Billy Graham Revival at Madison Square Garden

Hurricane Audrey Strikes U.S. Gulf Coast

Ford Promotes New Edsel

Kansas and Missouri Damaged by F5 Tornado

Hurricane Audrey brought winds in excess of 150 mph, causing immense damage to Texas and Louisiana. Despite warnings issued by the National Weather Service, many residents did not move to safety, resulting in over 400 fatalities.

National Headlines

Medical improvements

In 1957, handicapped children were now able to live more normal lives, thanks to the improvement of artificial limbs. The devices had been developed for adults, but had only recently become available to youth. Nylon, plastic and aluminum made the prostheses lighter. A new kind of continuing education was offered to doctors, and physicians could now keep up with medical developments by listening to recordings. Dentistry was a growing field, providing services that greatly improved oral hygiene.

Many diabetics were dependent on injections to control the symptoms of the disease. A new drug, tolbutamide in pill form, was developed and provided an alternative treatment to many.

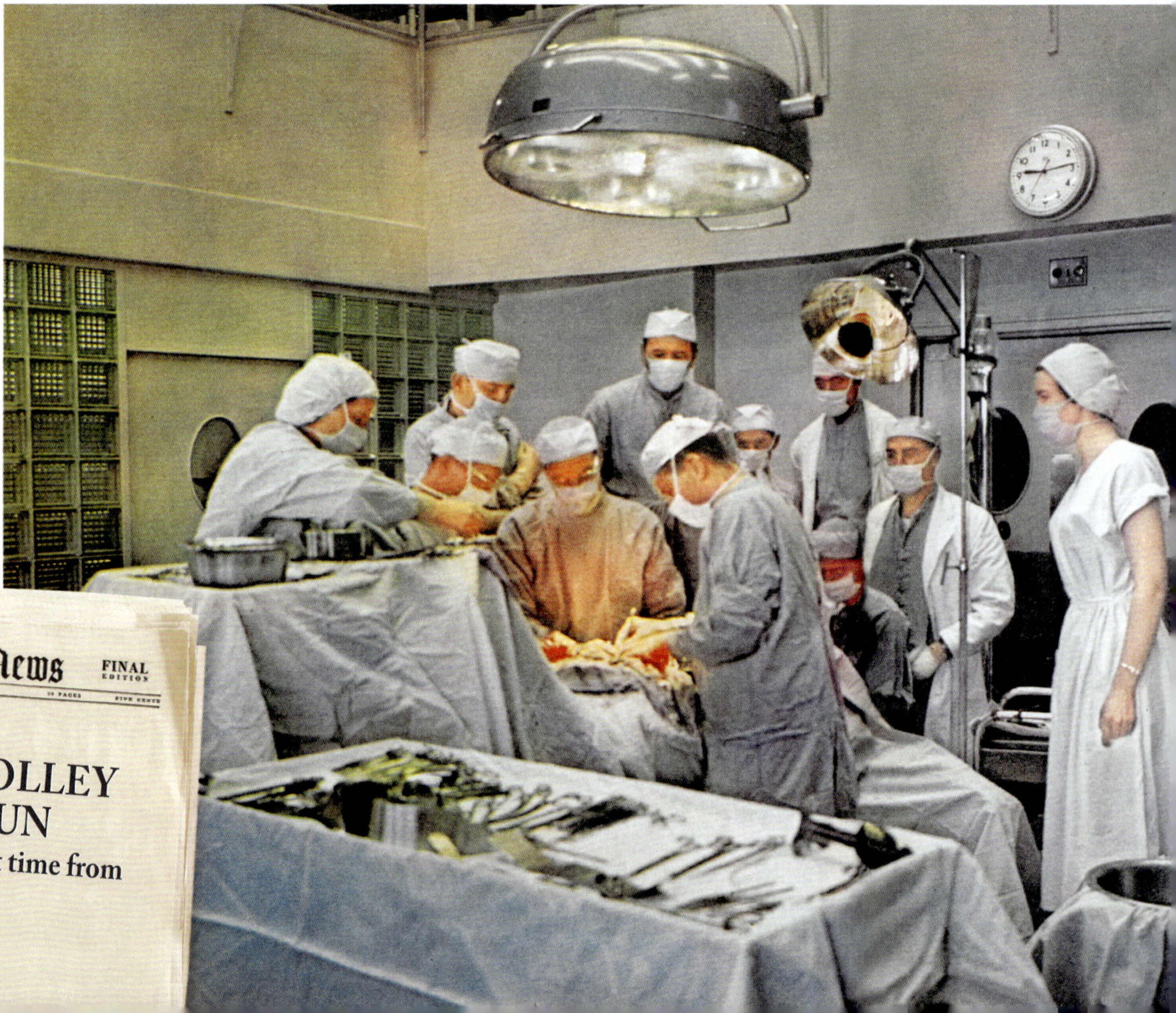

Special lamps that did not cast shadows improved operating-room lighting. This innovation was welcomed by doctors and nurses in hospitals across the country, helping relieve some of the tension of their vital jobs.

The Metro Daily News FINAL EDITION

APRIL 7, 1957

NYC ELECTRIC TROLLEY MAKES FINAL RUN

New York City trolley runs for last time from Queens to Manhattan.

Dentistry was booming. By 1957, nearly half of the school-age population visited the dentist about once a year.

Doctors could add to their medical knowledge more easily by listening to tape recordings rather than reading. They could listen while driving or during other daily activities.

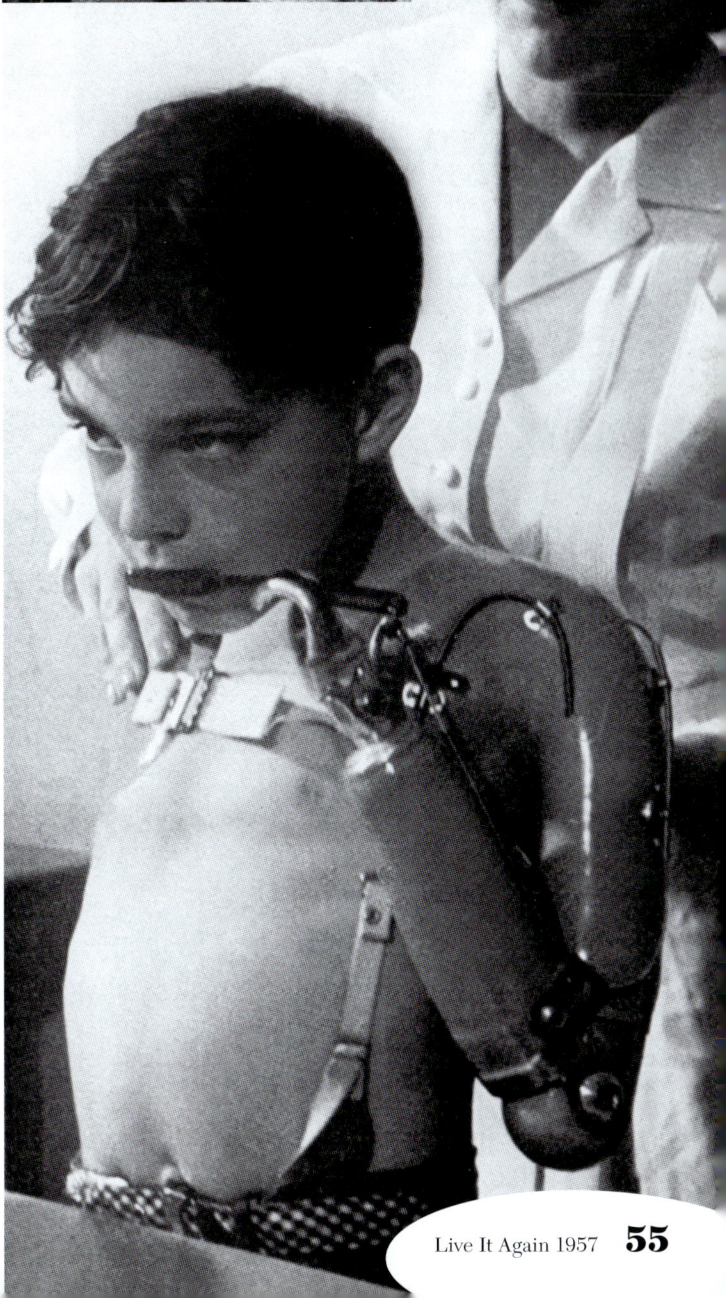

Just a few years before 1957, a handicapped child was dependent on others for care. The new lightweight, scaled-down versions of artificial limbs combined with improved physical therapy gave them freedom and a more normal lifestyle.

© GETTY IMAGES

Civil rights leader and Baptist minister Martin Luther King Jr. speaks on May 17 in support of the Civil Rights Bill of 1957, addressing thousands of people near the Reflecting Pool in Washington, D.C., during the Prayer Pilgrimage. It was the largest crowd King had ever addressed—about 30,000.

MEMORABLE QUOTE

"I have come to see more and more that one of the most decisive steps that the Negro can take is that little walk to the voting booth. That is an important step. We've got to gain the ballot, and through that gain, political power."

—Martin Luther King Jr., 1957

In September, federal court-ordered school integration reached Little Rock, Ark. The efforts to bring nine black students, the "Little Rock Nine," into an all-white school met with resistance. The Arkansas governor posted Arkansas National Guardsmen at the school to prevent the group from entering. All of this took place in front of journalists and national news cameras. President Eisenhower later sent the 101st Airborne Division to enforce the court order.

© GETTY IMAGES

National Headlines

Diversity efforts

Efforts to integrate African-Americans continued. The Prayer Pilgrimage was the first nationwide event to support the Civil Rights Bill and pressed for stronger measures. The demonstration was held in Washington, D.C. The bill was passed—the first of its kind in the century. In its original wording, the measure included investigation of abuses against black people and denial of the right to vote in southern states. However, the bill was amended to the point where the measure was mainly symbolic. In September, the "Little Rock Nine," a group of nine black students, were sent to desegregate all-white Central High School in Little Rock, Ark.

This African-American family was turned down by 70 trailer parks before a minister issued an appeal on their behalf to locate housing for the family.

Racial harmony reigned in a California community where white residents invited a black family to move into their neighborhood.

Students at a desegregated elementary school in Baltimore, Md., rehearse for their May Day Dance. The school board unanimously complied with integration, signaling a trend of lessening resistance.

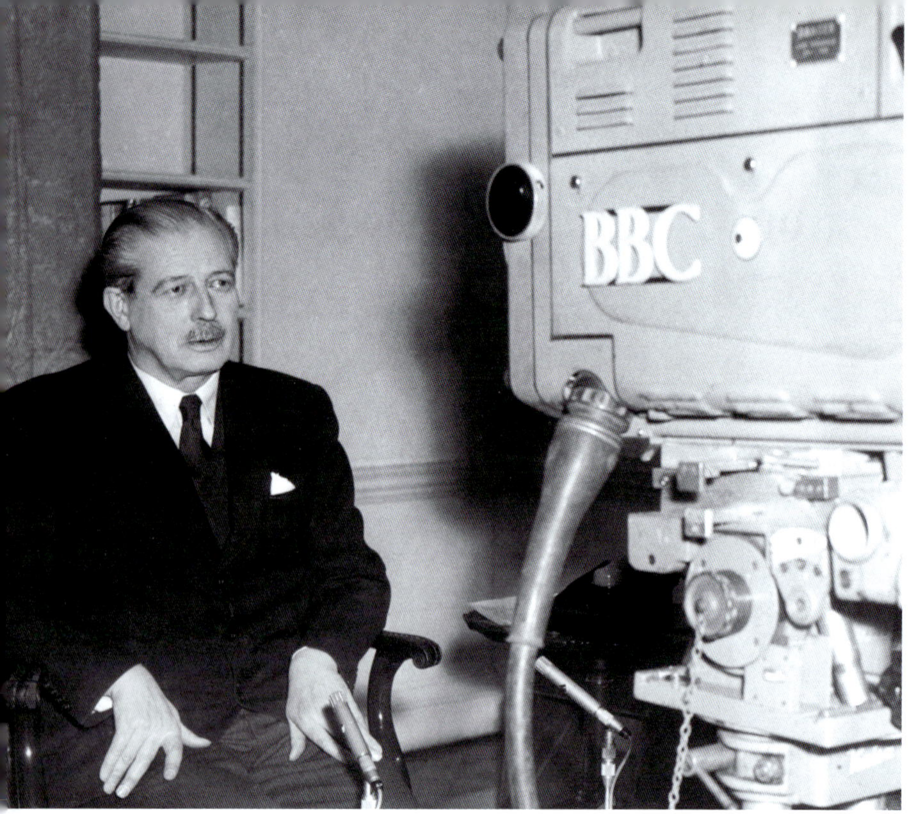

British Prime Minister Harold Macmillan records a political broadcast for the BBC. Under his leadership, former British colonies Ghana, Malaya and North Borneo were granted their independence.

World News

In January of 1957, Harold Macmillan became prime minister of the United Kingdom. Macmillan was a strong believer in social reform and the first Conservative prime minister to believe that countries under British rule should be given their freedom.

In March, the former Gold Coast British colony celebrated the end of 55 years of Western rule. The newly formed nation of Ghana was the first central African country to decolonize after the end of World War II.

Also in March, the European Common Market was formed between France, West Germany, Italy, Belgium, Luxembourg and the Netherlands. It was the first step toward European economic and political union.

FAMOUS BIRTHDAYS

Charles "Gadget" Jones, April 3 NBA forward (Houston Rockets)

Vince Gill, April 12 country musician

Soviet scientist Leonid I. Sedov, creator of Sputnik I, seated second from far right, attends a space conference. The launch of the Soviet satellite on October 4, 1957, marked the start of United States and Russian space race.

TTY IMAGES

World News

Outstanding Events

Ghana Becomes New African Nation

Harold Macmillan Named British Prime Minister

European Common Market Created

Sputnik I Launched by USSR

The Duchess of Kent reads a speech from the Queen of England to the National Assembly in Ghana, giving the Gold Coast its independence. During the period following World War II, many empires were reduced in size due to the immense costs of reconstruction of their war-torn countries.

1957 Trivia

Q. What town was Althea Gibson born in?

A. Silver, S.C.

© GETTY IMAGES

American tennis player Althea Gibson, right, is congratulated by fellow player Darlene Hard after she becomes the first African-American woman to win at Wimbledon. Even though she struggled with the same segregation issues that others dealt with at the time, she had an exciting career.

COURTESY OF MISS AMERICA ORGANIZATION

Marian McKnight of South Carolina was crowned Miss America. She was a high school valedictorian and straight-A college student.

Tennis player Lew Hoad was ranked in the World Top Ten for amateurs from 1952 until 1956. He became a professional player in 1957 and won at Wimbledon.

© GETTY IMAGES

1957 Titleholders

These winners transformed their areas of specialty and became national celebrities through the exposure. Althea Gibson was the first African-American to win major tennis championships. She had a great year in 1957, when she won the U.S. Open and Wimbledon. She also became the first of her race to be named Female Athlete of the Year by the Associated Press. Louise Suggs won the LPGA Championship. She was nicknamed "Miss Sluggs" by Bob Hope after he watched her ability to launch long drives. Australian Lew Hoad's movie-star looks and outgoing personality made him a popular tennis player in the 1950s. He turned pro in 1957 and won the Wimbledon championship.

Louise Suggs is captured mid-swing at the U.S. Open on her way to winning the LPGA Championship.

Doug Ford grew up playing both baseball and golf but chose to focus on golf, a good decision for the winner of the 1957 Masters Tournament.

1957 Titleholders

Proud champions

Bold Ruler, left, won the Preakness Stakes by two lengths and was named Horse of the Year in 1957. The horse was owned by Mrs. Gladys Mills Phipps of Wheatley Stable, one of the most successful thoroughbred farms in the nation.

Sam Hanks was the winner of the 1957 Indianapolis 500 with an average speed of 135.601 mph. He drove in the race 13 times, the most tries of any Indy winner. He announced his retirement from the racing circuit right after his win. The 200-lap race is often billed as "The Greatest Spectacle in Racing."

Bill Russell, 6-foot-10-inch Boston Celtics center, stands near coach Red Auerbach. Russell was named the NBA rebounding champion in 1957.

Sugar Ray Robinson, left, and Carmen Basilio, right, fight for the World Middleweight Title at Yankee Stadium in The Bronx, N.Y. Basilio went up a weight class to challenge Robinson and won an exciting 15-round decision.

The Boston Celtics, coached by Red Auerbach, were champions of the NBA in 1957, winning the best-of-seven series against the St. Louis Hawks, 4-3. It was Boston's first trip to the NBA Finals in the franchise's history.

1957 Titleholders

Conquering heroes

The 25th National Football League championship was played at Briggs Stadium in Detroit, Mich. The Detroit Lions were victorious 59-14 over the Cleveland Browns. In the center of this photo, Detroit Lions quarterback Tobin Rote, No. 18, throws a pass during the action.

Goalie Don Simmons of the Boston Bruins blocks a shot by Maurice Richard of the Montreal Canadiens during action of the 1957 Stanley Cup. The Canadiens won the series 4-1 for their second straight Cup victory.

The Milwaukee Braves won the 1957 World Series against the New York Yankees, four games to three. In the first inning of game 7, Yankee Hank Bauer dove back into second base, but was tagged out.

NATIONAL BASEBALL HALL OF FAME LIBRARY COOPERSTOWN, N.Y.

The Milwaukee Braves celebrate winning the World Series. The Yankees had dominated the American League with another lineup of superstars. Even though the Braves lacked a familiar roster of players, they were equally as dominant in the National League.

NATIONAL BASEBALL HALL OF FAME LIBRARY COOPERSTOWN, N.Y.

Henry "Hank" Aaron was the "big gun" outfielder of the Milwaukee Braves. He tallied 44 home runs and 132 runs batted in for a .322 average in only his fourth season and was the 1957 National League MVP.

The Metro Daily News

FINAL EDITION

20 PAGES

FIVE CENTS

MAY 28, 1957

BASEBALL'S NATIONAL LEAGUE AUTHORIZES TEAM MOVES

Decision made for Brooklyn Dodgers to relocate to Los Angeles and New York Giants to San Francisco.

Taking to the Road

Listening to the public's demand for more engine power and lower silhouettes, American automakers returned to manufacturing cars with more powerful engines and sleeker lines. The most successful company of the year was Chrysler. Each of the company's five lines featured torsion-bar suspension, dual headlights and push-button transmission. The biggest change in the industry was not in the cars, but the marketing. American companies recognized there was strong competition from European manufacturers and chose to sell imported products here instead of producing domestic competition.

COURTESY OF CHRYSLER GROUP LLC

Selling for $3,671, the De Soto Fireflite Sportsman 4-door hardtop offered high-powered luxury with a 295-horsepower motor.

REPRINTED WITH PERMISSION FROM FORD MOTOR CO.

Ford claimed to have built more cars with V-8 motors than the other automakers. The company's cars were advertised as the best because they had more time to test, improve and refine them. The Ford Fairline 500 Victoria sold for $2,381.

Station wagon sales boomed as the move to suburban areas continued.

REPRINTED WITH PERMISSION FROM GENERAL MOTORS CO.

Plymouth Suburban advertising claimed the station wagon was the biggest, longest and widest of its class.

REPRINTED WITH PERMISSION FROM THE WISCONSIN HISTORICAL SOCIETY & CNH AMERICA, LLC

The International Travelall could seat eight and was longer inside with more leg and headroom, yet shorter outside. The selling price of the station wagon was $2,364.

The Rambler solved the family car feud. The station wagon was easy to handle, yet also had big car room and comfort.

COURTESY OF CHRYSLER GROUP LLC

REPRINTED WITH PERMISSION FROM GENERAL MOTORS CO.

An advertisement for Chevrolet read, "No other low-priced car is quite so sweet, smooth and sassy, or so solidly and finely made." The Chevy Bel Air Sport 2-door coupe featured a new grille look and sold for $2,399.

Taking to the Road

Sporty cars

If you wanted fun and sport, as the advertisement read, there was no better and more exciting way to make your move than in a '57 Buick Century Convertible. The selling price was $3,598.

The Chrysler Imperial Crown Convertible offered fine engineering and superb ease of handling for $5,775.

"That's just one-third down and 24 backbreaking payments."

The Ford Skyliner convertible was the only hideaway hardtop that operated at the touch of a button, converting from steel-top sedan to open convertible in less than a minute. The huge trunk not only housed the steel roof, but left ample room for luggage too. The convertible sold for $2,942.

The Corvette ad said, "Chevrolet puts the 'purr in performance.' It's quiet as a contented cat, as smooth as cream and cat-quick in response," all for $3,465.

FAMOUS BIRTHDAYS

Scott Adams, June 8 cartoonist (creator of *Dilbert*)

Sterling Marlin, June 30 race car driver

There was a special kind of magic when driving a Swept-Wing Dodge convertible. The advertisement said, "You've never known a moment quite like this. When the night was so still and the air was so warm and the road was a velvet ribbon winding ahead. You sweep along in the peace and privacy of your own thoughts—your troubles a million miles away!"

Taking to the Road

Luxury cars

REPRINTED WITH PERMISSION FROM GENERAL MOTORS CO.

The Buick Roadmaster was the costliest of Buick's fine cars, but also the most distinguished with a low-sweep silhouette. Only Buick had the Safety-Minder device. You could just select the mph you wanted, and when you reached that pace, a warning buzzer sounded. Drop below that pace, and the buzzer stopped. The price ranged from $3,944 to $4,373.

REPRINTED WITH PERMISSION FROM GENERAL MOTORS CO.

The graceful, flowing lines of the 1957 Cadillac set it apart from other cars.

COURTESY OF CHRYSLER GROUP LLC

The Chrysler Windsor was a prestige car, yet in the $3,000 range, it could be purchased for the cost of most medium-priced cars. The resale value was at an all-time high too.

The Studebaker Golden Hawk had a built-in supercharger for more power when needed. It also had twin traction for driving power in both rear wheels.

The sweep and splendor of the Chrysler Imperial "sent a thunder of applause from coast to coast," read the advertisement. The luxury car came in eight models in a wide range of prices, from $4,586 to $6,898 depending on the model and equipment.

License plates varied in shape and size until 1956, when they were standardized to a size of 6 x 12 inches. This change allowed auto manufacturers to produce a uniform plate bracket.

Taking to the Road

Car maintenance

Car maintenance was easier in 1957. The engines were simpler and little was required to keep them running. Nearly anyone with a little mechanical ability could do the work themselves. A Ford truck could be purchased for less than $2,000 and ran on gas that cost about 24 cents a gallon. When it broke down, all that was required was a trip to the hardware store to buy a few supplies and a little elbow grease to do the repairs.

Most car owners were able to perform the oil changes themselves. People took pride in keeping their cars clean, washing and waxing them by hand. There were a few automatic car washes in the country, but owners were cautious of having their car finishes damaged by brushes.

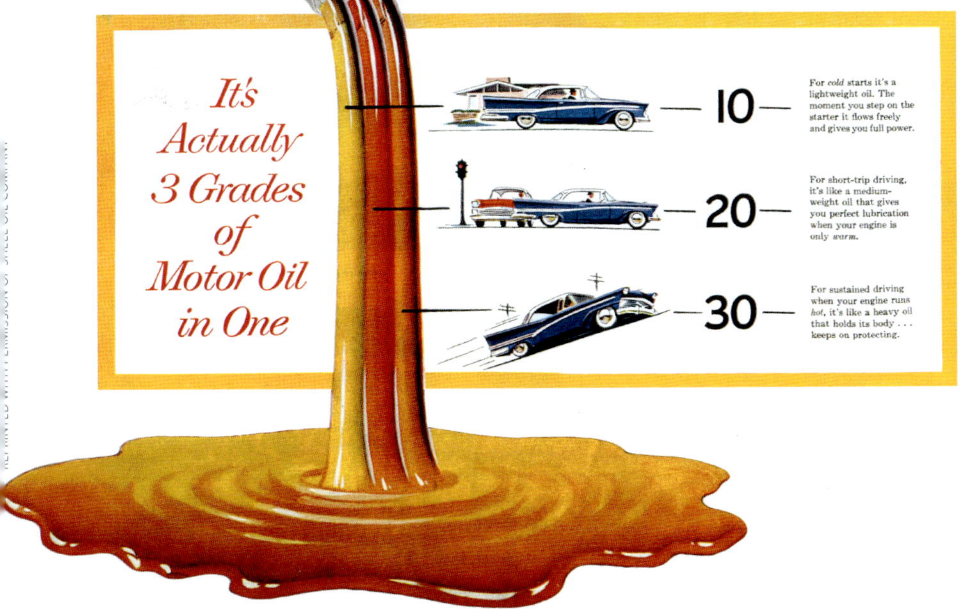

The Mackinac Bridge joined Michigan's lower and upper peninsulas. Construction of the bridge was completed in 1957, making it the longest suspension bridge in the world at the time. The suspension bridge itself, including anchoranges, is 8,614 feet long and the main towers rise 552 feet above the water. The cables weigh 11,849 tons. The bridge is a magnificent feat of engineering.

Building Our Superhighways

Across the country in both cities and rural areas, Americans made way for new highways. Lifestyles were changing and the desire to be more mobile resulted in more vehicles on the roads. The United States government passed the Federal-Aid Highway Act of 1956 to accommodate the demand for better roads. The act authorized the use of $25 billion for highway construction over a 13-year period beginning in 1957. Military and political leaders approved of this massive spending for national defense reasons as well. The new roads could more efficiently move troops and could also become airplane landing strips if needed.

New roads were being built across the country and through the mountains. People enjoyed watching the different phases of the construction.

"You don't have to worry about moving. The highway goes overhead at this point."

Many motorists headed to the country for their weekends, sometimes creating traffic jams. In Queens, N.Y., shown below, helicopters hover over the highways to spot congestion. From their aerial view, police officers could quickly spot trouble areas and send a tow truck or ambulance to the scene.

This scene of the construction of the Connecticut Turnpike graced the cover of *The Saturday Evening Post* on March 9, 1957. The new highways made it possible for drivers to commute to their jobs in less time.

FAMOUS BIRTHDAYS

Jon Lovitz, July 21 comic, actor

Wayne Grady, July 26 PGA golfer (1990 PGA Championship)

This man decides to make use of the train ride home from a business trip to calculate his expenses. Who knew entertaining the clients would cost so much?

A little humor lightens any day. This time the amusement arrives in the form of four grinning, mocking little boys who are fence sitting to watch Gramps get a ticket from the officer.

On one of the hottest days of the year, with temperatures hovering in the 90s, these sign painters are called upon to install a billboard advertising the cooling benefits of air conditioning!

Handyman Quiz

Test your skill on these wood-shop expressions as seen in a 1957 edition of *The Saturday Evening Post*.

1. Baluster	A. Abrasive
2. Cove	B. Vertical line
3. Riser	C. Stairway
4. Flute	D. Wood strip
5. Flint	E. Molding
6. Batten	F. Bolt
7. Bob	G. Railing
8. Drift	H. Drill

Answers: 1-G; 2-E; 3-C; 4-H; 5-A; 6-D; 7-B; 8-F

Making a Living

The process of earning a living changed from generation to generation. In 1957, many fathers had college degrees. Most of them drove to work and felt naked without their briefcases. Many of the college graduates just entering the job market wore suits to work, a symbol of the new professionalism. More women chose to work outside the home, especially after their children reached school age.

The discovery of confetti and a "Just Married" sign puts a twinkle in the eyes of these hotel maids.

FAMOUS BIRTHDAYS

Rod Langway, May 3 hockey player (Washington Capitals)

Judge Reinhold, May 21 actor

Telephone company workers enjoy this job location. Access to a sandy beach makes a perfect spot for lunch break.

"I keep getting myself."

Leading Ladies of *The Post*

Take a peek at some of the art inside the covers of *The Saturday Evening Post*. The Leading Ladies of *The Post* are a collection of images from regularly-featured steamy romance stories. Illustrators were challenged to interpret these stories on canvas and we have included a sampling of the Leading Ladies of 1957. The sultry fashion-forward heroines of the tales are featured along with the original article captions.

She had business in a strange city, and she didn't want her husband to tag along.

He wanted to marry Sharon, but there was a catch. First he had to find a husband for her sister.

The problem was to find a honeymooning actress who didn't want to be found.

Columbine stared at herself in the mirror. She was a beautiful woman, desirable, lovely in every way.

Her job was selling cars, and she had the best gimmick in the business.

Having $15 million and a penthouse makes it quite a bit easier for a girl to snag her man.

How can a wife keep her husband's love when her rival is younger and more beautiful?

These health and beauty products were among the many sold in 1957. Included are: Rayette Instant Aqua Tint hair coloring, Avon Cream Hair Lotion, Coppertone suntan lotion, Ipana Plus toothpaste, Super Anahist Antibiotic Throat Spray and Breck, Old Spice and Dial shampoos.

"What? You're 46? ... oh, come now, you're not serious ..."

Personal Products

Cosmetics for women were more popular than ever. The fashionable lady felt she must have penciled eyebrows, lashes emphasized with mascara and shiny, inviting lips. Most women received at least one perm in a lifetime. Many chose to do their perms at home instead of the hair salon. Aftershave lotions for men took the sting out of a shave and left behind a pleasing aroma. Mouthwash was a popular product for both men and women. No one wanted bad breath to disrupt their social lives!

Red and white were a popular color combination. The sailor-boy top and shorts were $6.77. The white swimsuit was flattering at any age and sold for $18.50.

1957 Style Trends

There was a delightful trend toward floral prints for spring of 1957. Femininity was enhanced with fashionable flower colors such as lilacs, peony pinks and larkspur blues, and the use of softer fabrics, floating panels and bloused backs. There were matching accessories in the Sears® catalog such as hosiery, jewelry, handbags, shoes and umbrellas. Suggestions were even given for accessories that matched swimsuits. There were "playsuits" for women, and shorts were called "shorties."

Playwear was prettier and more feminine. The outfit at left cost $9.94, the playsuit in the middle was $5.74 and the Bermuda shorts and shirt at right sold for $7.74.

The Metro Daily News

FINAL EDITION

JULY 15, 1957

NO. 1 ON THE CHARTS

"Teddy Bear" sung by Elvis Presley

The sweater and slim skirt at left in larkspur blue were priced together at $14.71. The dress at right was $9.70.

FAMOUS BIRTHDAYS

Melanie Griffith, August 9 actress

David Crane, August 10 film/TV producer (co-creator of *Friends*)

These models look radiant in bouquet prints. The floating panel dress at left was made of acetate taffeta and cost $10.70. The empire princess dress at right was trimmed with velvet ribbon and sold for $13.54.

Lightweight spring coats were $24 for the tweed on the left and also for the more fitted coat on the right.

The $7 wide-brimmed straw hat at right was circled with daisies. The dipping brim of the $10 hat below was heaped with lilac clusters.

The $5 diamond-weave straw hat above matched everything from suits to summer cottons.

With a crown almost hidden by roses, the $6 ripple-brim hat above was flirtatious and charming. The hat at left with a wide crown was $10.

Below, the tall draped hat in a basket shape sold for $4.97.

"We refer to our creations as amusing, not hilarious!"

1957 Style Trends

Fashion with "hattitude"

Nothing topped a lovely outfit quite like the perfect hat. Hats added the final touch of glamour to a woman's appearance. Last year's fashion find could easily be updated with new millinery or fresh ornaments like colorful ribbons, bows, flowers or tulle. Many hats were small and worn close to the head. Others had broader brims and were decked with flowers. The hats on these pages reflect the variety of the fashions of 1957.

This woman is so excited about her "darling" new Easter hat that she even wakes in the middle of the night to admire it.

A wide-brimmed hat provided protection from the sun as well as being a fashion statement.

1957 Style Trends

Men's attire

1957 AMERICAN INSTITUTE OF MEN & BOYS' WEAR

A 1957 ad by the American Institute of Men and Boys' Wear gave good fashion advice. It read, "The way you look has much to do with the way that people look at you. Put pride in your stride. Pay attention to your clothes, and you'll feel right because you'll look right—in clothes that fit, in colors that match, in a hat that's up-to-date. What you wear is as much a part of the impression you make as your smile, your voice, your handshake."

More advice about looking good in 1957 was: "Dressing right means looking right, whatever the occasion, all through the day. Even in the rain. Even in your own backyard. Even in pajamas or underwear (your wife deserves a break, too, doesn't she!)."

1957 AMERICAN INSTITUTE OF MEN & BOYS' WEAR

1957 AMERICAN INSTITUTE OF MEN & BOYS' WEAR

1957 AMERICAN INSTITUTE OF MEN & BOYS' WEAR

Jarman air-cooled shoes were smartly styled in premium leathers, lightweight for easy walking and priced from $9.95 to $18.95 for most styles.

Even at the golf course, dressing right is a habit that pays off in both comfort and self-assurance. First notice what looks good on others. Then identify the styles that look the best on you.

"It only comes in three other ghastly colors."

Feel like a new man with a new suit. A new pair of slacks and jacket can make you look and feel like a million bucks. A suit topped off with a hat was typical office attire in 1957.

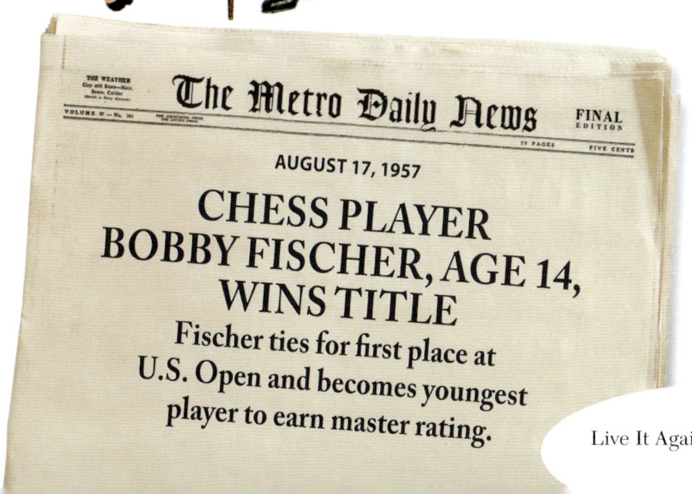

The Metro Daily News

FINAL EDITION

AUGUST 17, 1957

CHESS PLAYER BOBBY FISCHER, AGE 14, WINS TITLE

Fischer ties for first place at U.S. Open and becomes youngest player to earn master rating.

Warm weather isn't needed to enjoy the great outdoors during a date. Gliding across the ice side-by-side is so romantic until feet get tangled, and then down the couple goes in a laughing heap.

"Golly, what a great day for a picnic! I'll bring the franks, you bring the rolls," he exclaims. "I just love being with you, dear, even when we are in places where ants are likely to attack!" she replies. It's amazing how young love can gloss over discomforts for the sake of romance.

Matters of the Heart

Life is full of surprises. You never know who may be just around the next corner. The day may start out the same as always, and then unexpectedly, a boy meets a girl, and the sparks fly. So, as they get to know one another, a couple may feel as though they are alone, even in a crowded world.

Meeting and dating that special someone is the stuff of dreams, among the highlights of life.

"May I kiss you good night, Dorothy? Alice? Elizabeth?"

Listen in to what might have been a typical boy/girl conversation from 1957:

He said: And have you heard about the disc jockey who lives on spins and needles?

She said: Oh no! A zero on the laugh-meter for you, boy!

He said: No charge, Marge. It's free glee!

She said: My grandma tells 'em better—and I'm not braggin'!

The Metro Daily News

FINAL EDITION

SEPTEMBER 29, 1957

GREEN BAY PACKERS DEFEAT CHICAGO BEARS IN NEW STADIUM

The City Stadium was completed just in time to host the season opener for a 21-17 victory over the Bears. The stadium was renamed Lambeau Field in 1965.

Matters of the Heart

Tying the knot

Many brides of the 1950s kept the old tradition of wearing "something old, something new, something borrowed, something blue." Something old symbolized a link to family and the past, such as an heirloom. Wearing something new represented a wonderful new life. Something borrowed stood for the love and support of family and friends. Something blue, such as a garter or ribbon, symbolized faithfulness and loyalty.

The details of planning the wedding are finished. The bride can now breathe a sigh of relief and concentrate on the vows. Her groom, dressed in his best, is stunned by the beauty of his bride.

Important fashions for important occasions could be found in a Sears® catalog. The wedding dress at left with its many layers of lace sold for $30. The bridesmaid dress at right cost $18.50.

Actors Natalie Wood and Robert Wagner were wed on Dec. 28, 1957, in Scottsdale, Ariz.

The wedding was a grand celebration. Now it's time for the couple to make their great escape, though many will notice their departure with streamers flying and old shoes clattering and banging behind the car.

Movie Trivia

Q. What character did Natalie Wood play in *Miracle on 34th Street?*

A. Susan Walker, the adorable little girl who learned to believe in Santa Claus.

"Whoops!"

Brides and grooms of the 1950s often opened their gifts during the reception instead of waiting until after the honeymoon.

The couple dated, became engaged, exchanged wedding rings and enjoyed a wonderful honeymoon, just a few of the "firsts" they will enjoy as they journey down life's road.

AMOS SEWELL

Family Life

"When we recall the past, we usually find that it is the simplest things—not the great occasions—that in retrospect give off the greatest glow of happiness," said comedian Bob Hope. And so it is with family life. American society in 1957 was geared toward the family; marriage and children were the centers of life.

A new addition to the family inspires many different feelings. Dad is proud, Mom is thrilled and big brother is awed by the whole proceedings.

First birthdays are supposed to be all about smiles and that sweet first taste of cake. Junior loudly proclaims his birthday wish that everyone would just go away so he can nap!

"Well, what kind of day has it been?"

Family Life
Full of surprises

Part of the fun of Christmas is anticipation and spying on parents to discover where the gifts are stashed.

When Mom comes down those stairs, what will she notice first, the handmade Mother's Day card, or the muddy tracks left behind by son and dog? Children do manage to keep life interesting.

"Dad, your boss is here already! Mom, come downstairs now!" shouts the little boy. Having the boss and his wife over for dinner seemed like such a good idea at the time.

FAMOUS BIRTHDAYS

Gloria Estefan, September 1
singer, songwriter (The Miami Sound Machine)

Fran Drescher, September 30
actress (*The Nanny*)

There is plenty in the backyard to entertain a child. But is the swing set the first choice? No, the forbidden flowers look far more appealing.

"Watch them, they're small but they operate well as a team."

The hostess worked long and hard on food preparation for the party, making sure every detail was perfect. What was unexpected was the entrance of the family dog, who also thought the food looked irresistible.

The Metro Daily News
FINAL EDITION

OCTOBER 17, 1957

ENGLAND'S QUEEN ELIZABETH II ARRIVES IN WASHINGTON, D.C., FOR STATE VISIT

The Queen also visits Canada.

The 1957 Home

The family room became an important space in the homes built in 1957. There was a demand for sturdy, comfortable furniture for this room that often housed the family television. Interior color schemes were simple and subdued, with turquoise and pink chosen as the most popular colors. The majority of floors were covered with easy-care vinyl.

The suburban ranch with a large picture window on the street side and attached one-car garage was the most popular style for new houses built in 1957.

This split-level dream house became more of a nightmare when the $29,995 price tag was revealed. The average new home in 1957 cost $12,220, less than half the selling price of this ultra-modern dwelling.

There was something warm and friendly about using natural materials like wood and brick when decorating an informal family room. Pink was a popular color choice for sturdy cast-iron and china bathtubs, sinks and toilets. Vinyl tile floors were ideal for playrooms. A damp mopping was all that was required to clean the surface.

Available in General Electric Mix-or-Match colors—or white.

TOUCH . . . and the vegetable bins revolve. Vegetables and fruits ride right out in front of you!

Revolving Shelves, Magnetic Door, Big New Roll-Out Freezer

This two-burner Frigidaire fold-back surface unit lifted out of the way when not in use, making it a wonderful space saver.

The built-in French-door wall oven by Frigidaire took less aisle space.

A built-in countertop stove could be put nearly anywhere and expanded kitchen design possibilities.

The 1957 Home

Appliances

Built-in appliances made dream kitchens come true. The glamorous new styles had all the most requested time- and work-saving features. The modern concept of appliances that fit evenly with cabinets eliminated space-wasting bulges and dust-trap gaps. "Shove out the old look and slip in the sheer look," proclaimed a Frigidaire advertisement. Most appliances were available in mix-or-match colors and the traditional white. The sides, top and back of the new refrigerator-freezers were flat so they could be flush against a wall or fit neatly into a corner.

Westinghouse unveiled the new Space-Mates, a stacked washer and dryer that was only 25 inches wide.

During Frigidaire's "Color Carnival of Values" advertising campaign, appliances were sold in colors including pink, yellow and the smart new charcoal gray. The four women in this advertisement are all making the sign for Frigidaire's "Sheer Look" logo—appliances that fit square with cabinets.

FAMOUS BIRTHDAYS

Bernie Mac, October 5 comic, actor (*The Bernie Mac Show*)

Martin Luther King III, October 23 activist

The 1957 Home

Homemaker's helpers

Take the short quiz on the facing page and discover how your kitchen of today measures up with those of 1957. An amazing number of time-saving gadgets burst onto the market during the prosperous 1950s that homemakers during the Great Depression of the 1930s and war-rationing years of the 1940s would ever have dreamed possible.

West Bend sold a wide variety of gadgets, including a $27.95 automatic griddle, $7.95 electric corn popper and $6.95 electric buffet server, now known as a slow cooker

How does your kitchen rate on the electrical living scale?

Is your kitchen really up-to-date? You may get some surprises, and some good ideas, too, when you check it on the Live Better Electrically "Kitchen Scale" below. There are so many wonderful new ways to put electricity to work in your kitchen today—tireless new electric servants that give you more time and energy for yourself and your family. Decide now which of these electrical work savers you need first. They're easier to buy than you may realize. See your local electrical dealer or utility for the pleasant details.

How many of these electric appliances do you own?

- ____ Dishwasher
- ____ Mixer
- ____ Electric Range
- ____ Juicer
- ____ Refrigerator-Freezer
- ____ Waste Disposer
- ____ Chafing Dish
- ____ Food Blender
- ____ Food Freezer
- ____ Skillet
- ____ Electric Clothes Dryer
- ____ Broiler-Rotisserie
- ____ Work-Surface Lighting
- ____ Air Conditioner
- ____ Toaster
- ____ Full HOUSEPOWER (Adequate Wiring)
- ____ Timer
- ____ Casserole
- ____ Automatic Washer
- ____ Counter-Top Cooking Unit
- ____ Food Slicer
- ____ Electric Water Heater
- ____ Deep-Fat Fryer
- ____ Electronic Oven
- ____ Bean Pot
- ____ Enough Outlets
- ____ Grill
- ____ Roll Warmer
- ____ Kettle
- ____ Ventilating Fan
- ____ Built-In Oven
- ____ Coffee Maker
- ____ Electric Pressure Cooker

Circle total here

24 23 22 21 20 19 | 18 17 16 15 14 13 | 12 11 10 9 8 7 | 6 5 4 3 2 1

Here's how your kitchen rates!

24–19: *Just wonderful!*
You've arrived! Your kitchen works instead of you. Now you're really living better electrically!

18–13: *Enjoyable!*
You're in clover with electricity doing so much of the work. But look what you're still missing.

12–7: *Bearable!*
You're still tied to those kitchen apron strings; but with more electrical aids, living is so much easier!

6–1: *Roughing it!*
So few appliances to help you. No wonder you're so tired when day's done!

FREE IDEA BOOK
—hundreds of practical hints for making life pleasanter, easier. Ask for "Ideas to Help You Live Better . . . Electrically" at your local electric utility.

LIVE BETTER ...Electrically

LIVE BETTER ELECTRICALLY

Before 1934, there were an estimated 500 pizzerias in the United States. In 1957, the number of pizza restaurants rose to about 20,000, selling pizzas that cost anywhere from 65 cents to $5. The pizza below was prepared using a Chef Boy-Ar-Dee mix.

Heinz made five different kinds of beans. A favorite meal was a combination of beans, barbecued spareribs and a mixed green salad. Beans were also good with hot dogs.

7UP and other sparkling sodas were the perfect complement to sandwiches or a large plate of burgers and beans.

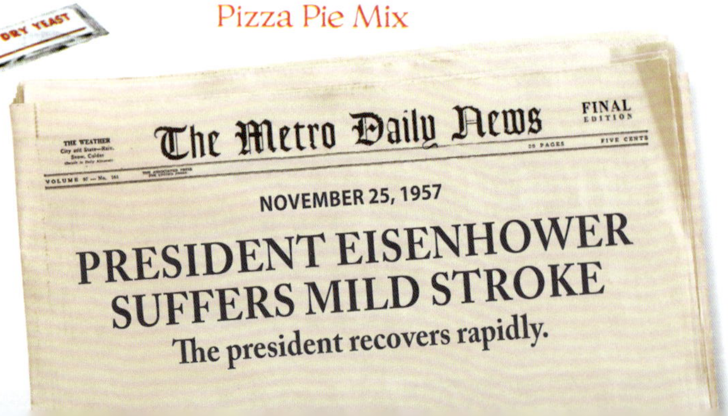
The Metro Daily News

FINAL EDITION

NOVEMBER 25, 1957

PRESIDENT EISENHOWER SUFFERS MILD STROKE

The president recovers rapidly.

Favorite Foods

Foods transitioned from the basic meat and potatoes meals of the 1940s to burgers with fries and a variety of ethnic foods that became popular in the 1950s. Recipes for "Americanized" versions of chow mein, lasagna and sukiyaki began to appear in cookbooks. People were crazy about pizza, the tasty Italian concoction that was a close contender to the hot dog as a favorite snack. Cooking on the backyard barbecue became a popular suburban trend.

Noodles combined with Dinty Moore® Beef Stew makes a tasty meal. The stew, made of lean beef, tender carrots and firm white potatoes in a rich gravy, is a quick and easy dish.

Foods taste even better with thick, tangy catsup. Even though it takes awhile for the condiment to come out of the bottle, it's worth the wait.

"Put on some tangos, we're having Spanish Rice."

What Made Us Laugh

"I think she's going to regret marrying a doctor."

"The champ seems to be biding his time."

"I'm originally a Route 107 girl and my husband is from the Jersey Turnpike."

"Ouch! I'll take them!"

"This should be interesting."

"It's fragile—so throw it underhand, please."

"Don't count on him finding our house. He couldn't even remember the names of his reindeer!"

Free-Time Fillers

A leisure activity can be defined as time spent away from cares and daily responsibilities. These are the moments when we are free to choose what makes us happiest. Each person is unique, and so are the ways we choose to fill our free time. During the warm months, some enjoy golfing, baseball or horseback riding. When it's cold outside, the action usually moves indoors with table games, cards, music and books. In the winter, hardier souls choose to go ice fishing, sledding or skating.

Some folks can't get enough of fishing in the warmer months, so they extend the season to winter. Ice fishing is a chilly adventure, unless using one of those cozy and warm shacks.

Men are too intense about their golf games. Perhaps they should learn from these ladies and play at a more leisurely pace. Never mind that play on the fairway is backed up at least three holes as other golfers sit down to wait.

"Maybe you should try a lighter ball."

Which one is more nervous about this attempt at horseback riding, the girl or the horse?

This is a painting of Yogi Berra, catcher of the New York Yankees, who is intent upon catching a foul ball. The illustration was the cover of *The Saturday Evening Post* for the April 20, 1957, edition.

Bridge and Canasta, also known as Basket Rummy, were popular card games for groups.

Music is the center point of this relaxed group activity.

FAMOUS BIRTHDAYS

Lyle Lovett, November 1 country musician, actor

Caroline Kennedy, November 27 daughter of President John F. and Jackie Kennedy

In 1957, Greyhound bus lines introduced its goodwill ambassador, "Lady Greyhound." The dog wearing a jeweled crown appeared at a number of events nationwide for the next decade.

The Northern Pacific's famous train, the Vista-Dome North Coast Limited, offered many extras for pleasant travel including great views and a buffet lounge.

Modes of Transportation

Americans traveled in record numbers in 1957. Winter tourists descended on the Caribbean, arriving by ship or plane. Due to increased travel, new airport terminals were being built across the country to provide access for new larger airplanes. Air travel that had not changed since World War II was now in the beginning stages of the jet age. About 40 million people visited the national parks, enjoying America's wide variety of natural wonders. Busses proved to be a reliable, less costly service for many people. Bus companies added extra-fare runs to pamper passengers with hostesses and free lunches, believing they would be more competitive with trains and planes for long-distance travel.

The TWA Jetstream offered "the quiet of anti-vibration propellers, the smoothness of giant wings and the sureness of electronic-eye radar" that made a trip by plane seem hours shorter.

This is a photo of Chicago's O'Hare airport as it appeared in 1957.

More than a million passengers traveled to Europe in 1957 via airplane or luxury liner, as illustrated in this Samsonite luggage advertisement.

Out for a drive to enjoy the fresh air and sunshine, these boys stumble upon unexpected scenery and decide to venture to the pool instead.

Vacation Fun

In 1957, we could travel almost anywhere, thanks to cars, jetliners, ships, buses and trains. The new highways made it easy for families to visit amusement parks and take in the scenic beauty of one of the national parks. For the people who could afford it, air travel was considered the most glamorous option.

"Thank heaven! Now our vacation starts!"

Waterskiing was once an activity mostly for those lucky enough to live on a lake. In the 1950s, the sport became popular. People rented lakeside vacation cottages and enjoyed many hours on the water.

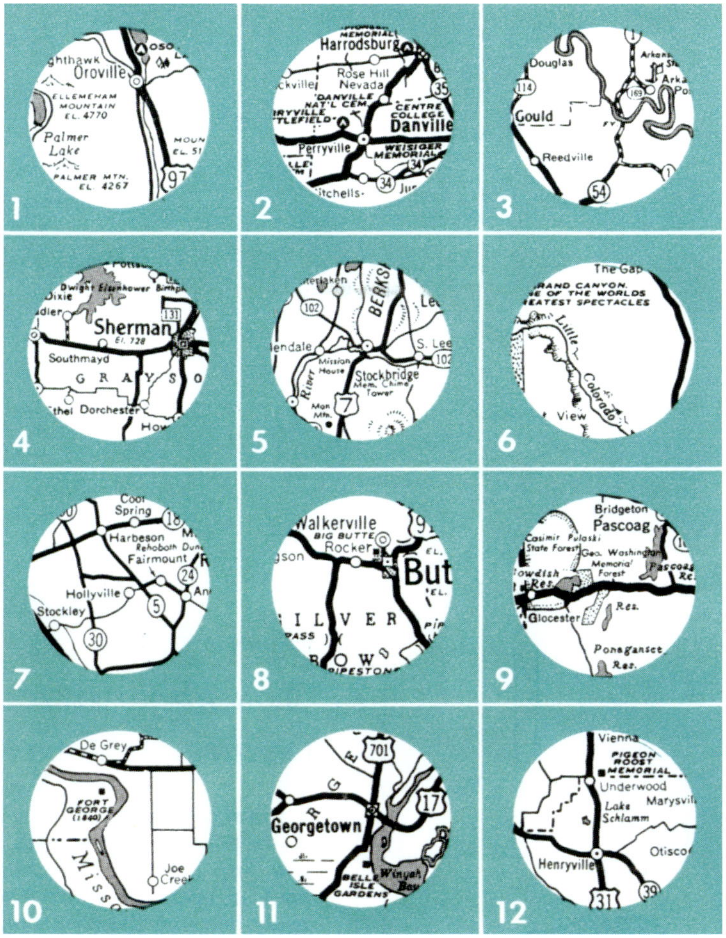

Where Do You Think You Are?

East or west, north or south, each of the distinctive areas above appeared on the road map of a single state in 1957. There is, as the saying goes, "no place like it." Can you identify the states?

Answers: 1-Washington; 2-Kentucky; 3-Arkansas; 4-Texas; 5-Massachusetts; 6-Arizona; 7-Delaware; 8-Montana; 9-Rhode Island; 10-South Dakota; 11-South Carolina; 12-Indiana

Children were thrilled by the rides at amusement parks such as Coney Island in Brooklyn, N.Y.

While the rest of the family goes on vacation, the poor family dog must make do with the local kennel. While he may feel abandoned for a time, the reunion at vacation's end will be joyous.

Alta, Utah, was one of the most popular ski areas in the United States. Ski enthusiasts, both young and old, enjoyed snow at the resort from Thanksgiving until May.

Girls dressed in white participated in a graduation-day ceremony at Anna Head School in Berkeley, Calif. Schools across the country celebrated the milestone event in different ways.

The people of Pomfret, Vt., paid $1.25 to eat their fill of a yearly traditional turkey supper. The occasion combined the scents of homemade food with the conversations of neighbors.

The Face of America

The Saturday Evening Post ran a series of articles called The Face of America in the magazine. The photographs showcased the immense diversity to be found in America. Ranging from ordinary activities such as a school recess or yearly harvest to special events including fireworks and snow-skiing trips, the photos captured Americans at their best.

When summer heated up in Boston, residents flocked to the Frog Pond on the Common to cool off. Splashing in the fountain was a fun way to deal with hot temperatures.

Outside Frontenac School in southeastern Minnesota, children joined hands while playing ring around the rosie. This one-room schoolhouse was one of only a few that remained.

Some 400 energetic students attended a dance celebrating graduation at the Paul D. Schreiber High School in Port Washington, N.Y. The party lasted throughout the night.

The Face of America

At noon during wheat harvest in Logan and Gove counties, Kan., the combines were halted in favor of food. This area of Kansas was known as "the buckle of the wheat belt."

On a cattle operation near Springer, N.M., a group of Boy Scouts were given the once-in-a-lifetime opportunity to assist with roundup. Experienced cowhands included the boys during branding.

In Madison Square Garden in New York City, over a hundred dog breeds were on display for the chance to win ribbons and trophies at the Westminster Kennel Club show.

Folks in Memphis, Tenn., threw a huge party in honor of cotton, the South's cloth of gold. The yearly festival included a week of parades, fireworks, fancy balls and fashion shows.

A cluster of costumed little sprites visited a home in Schenectady, N.Y. "Trick or treat!" they cried and were given all types of goodies during their round of the neighborhood.

The nation's largest post-office building in 1957 was located in Chicago, Ill. As the holidays approached, workers sorted through the mountain of packages around the clock.

At the 809 Club on Bourbon Street in New Orleans, La., a woman demonstrated the moves of Latin-American specialty dances such as the calypso, the mambo and the cha-cha.

Santa takes time from his Christmas Eve deliveries to be sure the toys are all in working order on this cover of the *Jack and Jill* magazine, a favorite for kids.

Christmas Traditions

Decorating the tree was one of the high points of a holly jolly Christmas. Many trees were freshly cut and filled the air with the scent of pine. Remember those older-model tree stands? Getting the tree to stand upright in the holder could be quite a challenge, even for Dad. The yearly untangling of the Christmas lights that involved the whole family often led to rounds of laughter. Decorations, each bringing back a special memory, were hung on the branches with care.

Christmas is a time to attend holiday parties. With so many delectable dishes on display, it is difficult to sample them all.

The Metro Daily News

FINAL EDITION

DECEMBER 14, 1957

TV CARTOON SHOW *RUFF AND REDDY* DEBUTS

This Saturday morning show is hosted by Jimmy Blaine and created by animators William Hanna and Joseph Barbera.

The spirit of Christmas shone through the windows of both country and city churches as special services celebrated the birth of Christ.

While cutting wood to keep the home fires warm and bright, a Christmas tree is also brought to the house for decorating.

As they woke Christmas morning, children rushed to their stockings to discover presents brought by Santa. Wearing matching pajamas added to the Christmas cheer.

Perfect gift ideas for men included $6.50 slip-on leather shoes, a shirt and tie set priced at $3.98 and leather gloves lined with rabbit fur that sold for $7.50.

1957 MONTGOMERY WARD

1957 MONTGOMERY WARD

Gifts that would appeal to boys included a $3.98 coat sweater, ranger axe and knife kit for $3.95 and junior all-star football set for $4.98.

Some of the delightfully feminine gifts for women were a $5.49 vanity mirror, a $5.95 lacy slip and a pajama set for $5.95.

1957 MONTGOMERY WARD

Christmas Traditions

Gift giving

One focus of the season was locating that perfect gift that would bring smiles to cherished faces on Christmas day. The mail-order catalog was a good place to start when looking for gift ideas. Shoppers were advised to avoid forgetting someone during the last-minute shopping rush by buying presents early.

FAMOUS BIRTHDAYS

Donny Osmond, December 9 talk-show host, actor, musician (*Donny and Marie* TV show)

Ray Romano, December 21 comic, actor (*Everybody Loves Raymond*)

Matt Lauer, December 30 talk-show host (*Today Show*)

1957 MONTGOMERY WARD

A swing-style skirt with cute appliques was all the rage and made many a girl's Christmas wish list. This blouse and skirt set was priced at $5.98.

Fashionable gifts for girls included a $2.98 party slip, $2.19 shoulder bag and a Betsy McCall beauty-aid set for $3.59.

1957 MONTGOMERY WARD

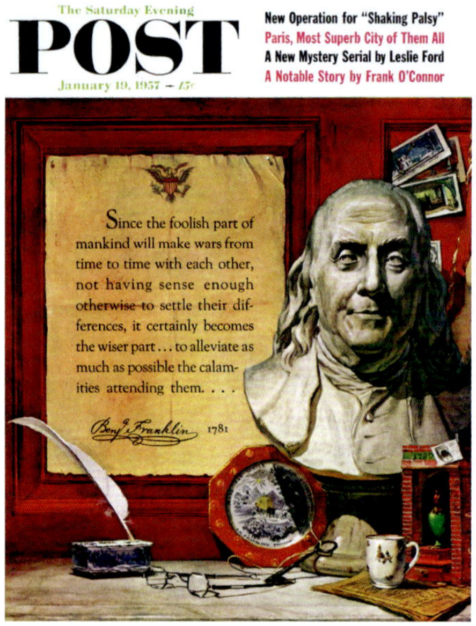

More *The Saturday Evening Post* Covers

The Saturday Evening Post covers were works of art, many illustrated by famous artists of the time, including Norman Rockwell. Most of the 1957 covers have been incorporated within the previous pages of this book; the few that were not are presented on the following pages for your enjoyment.

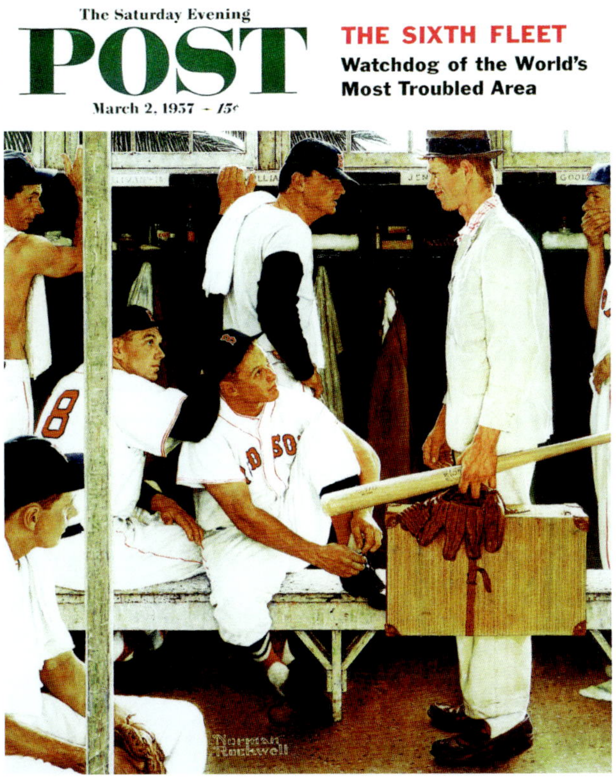
The Saturday Evening
POST
March 2, 1957 – 15¢
THE SIXTH FLEET
Watchdog of the World's
Most Troubled Area
Norman Rockwell

The Saturday Evening
POST
March 30, 1957 – 15¢
THE LADY COPS OF THE DOPE SQUAD
The Yankees are Wondering:
Is Larsen a One-Game Flash?

The Saturday Evening
POST
April 6, 1957 – 15¢
Is France Still Our Ally?
By Ernest O. Hauser
Taxpayer's Ordeal:
"BRING ALL YOUR
CANCELED CHECKS..."

The Saturday Evening
POST
May 4, 1957 – 15¢
THE WAIFS
By WILLIAM FAULKNER
From His New Novel, The Town
How Hodge of Illinois
Stole the State's Millions
A Novelette
By WILLIAM SAROYAN
SUNNY JIM FITZSIMMONS:
"I Like the Kentucky Derby, But—"

The Saturday Evening
POST
May 18, 1957 — 15¢
The Fabulous Jock Whitney
By RICHARD THRUELSEN
BASEBALL'S GOT ME!
By Gussie Busch
of the St. Louis Cardinals

The Saturday Evening
POST
June 1, 1957 — 15¢
Jayne Mansfield:
ANYTHING
FOR PUBLICITY

The Saturday Evening
POST
June 15, 1957 — 15¢
THE DEEP SOUTH
SAYS "NEVER!"
The Hard Facts
About "Integration"
By JOHN BARTLOW MARTIN
TV'S WYATT EARP
By PETE MARTIN
NO STOPPING
NEXT EXIT
32 MI.
NO U TURN
ROUTE M-20

The Saturday Evening
POST
September 14, 1957 – 15¢
BIRDS OF OUR LAND
An Eight-Page Portfolio
of Photographs in Full Color

The Saturday Evening
POST
October 12, 1957 – 15¢
THE NEGRO
IN THE NORTH
By CARL T. ROWAN
The Woes of West Coast Football

The Saturday Evening
POST
November 16, 1957 – 15¢
Daredevils
of the Golden Gate
STOP US
BEFORE WE KILL AGAIN
BY A RACING DRIVER
FASHIONS BY SYBIL CONNOLLY

MORE FAMOUS BIRTHDAYS

January 4
Patty Loveless, country singer

January 6
Nancy Lopez, LPGA golfer

January 12
John Lasseter, film director (*Toy Story*)

January 19
Ottis Anderson, running back (New York Giants)

January 23
Princess Caroline of Monaco, daughter of Prince Rainier and Princess Grace Kelly

January 27
Frank Miller, cartoonist, author (*The Dark Knight Returns*)

January 28
Harley Jane Kozak, actress, novelist
Nick Price, PGA golfer

January 29
Irlene Mandrell, country musician (The Mandrell Sisters)

February 7
Carney Lansford, baseball player (Oakland Athletics)

February 13
Denise Austin, fitness expert

February 15
Jimmy Spencer, race car driver (NASCAR)

February 19
Dave "Smoke" Stewart, pitcher (Oakland Athletics)
Ray Winstone, actor (*Vincent*)

February 28
Paul Delph, musician, producer
John Turturro, actor (*Barton Fink, Five Corners*)

March 7
Robert Harris, author (*Fatherland*)

March 11
Cheryl Lynn, soul and disco vocalist

March 12
Marlon Jackson, musician (The Jackson Five)

March 15
Park Overall, actress (*Empty Nest*)
Joaquim de Almeida, actor (*Clear and Present Danger*)

March 20
Theresa Russell, actress (*Insignificance* and *Black Widow*)
Vanessa Bell Calloway, actress (*Coming to America*)

March 30
Paul Reiser, actor (*Mad About You*)
Michael Lehmann, film director (*Heathers*)

March 31
Marc McClure, actor (*Superman: The Movie*)

April 8
Fred Smerlas, football player (Buffalo Bills)

April 11
John Castellanos, actor (John Silva of *The Young & the Restless*)

April 13
Amy Goodman, radio personality, journalist (host of *Democracy Now!*)

April 15
Evelyn Ashford, sprinter (Olympic gold medalist)

April 17
Teri Austin, actress (Jill Bennett of *Knots Landing*)

April 23
Jan Hooks, comic (*Saturday Night Live*)

April 29
Daniel Day-Lewis, actor (*My Left Foot*)

April 30
Duane G. "Digger" Carey, NASA astronaut

May 8
Bill Cowher, former football coach (Pittsburgh Steelers)

May 10
Phil Mahre, alpine skier (1984 Olympic gold medalist)

May 13
Alan Ball, screenwriter (*American Beauty*)

May 19
Bill Laimbeer, basketball center (Detroit Pistons)

May 23
Mark Arnold, actor (Joe Perkins of *Santa Barbara*)

May 28
Kirk Gibson, outfielder (Detroit Tigers, Los Angeles Dodgers)
Ben Howland, basketball coach (UCLA)

May 29
Charles Robert "Bobby" Hamilton Sr., race car driver (NASCAR)

May 31
Jim Craig, goaltender (1980 Olympic gold medalist)

June 1
Jeff Hawkins, computer programmer (inventor of the Palm Pilot and Treo)

June 9
T.D. Jakes, televangelist

June 12
Timothy Busfield, actor (Elliot Weston of *Thirtysomething*)

June 14
Jay Roach, film/TV director (*Austin Powers: International Man of Mystery*)

June 21
Berke Breathed, cartoonist (*Bloom County*)

June 23
Frances McDormand, actress (Marge Gunderson of *Fargo*)

July 2
Bret "Hitman" Hart, WCW wrestler

July 9
Kelly McGillis, actress (*Top Gun*)

July 16
Faye Grant, actress (Dr. Julie Parrish of *V*)

July 20
Donna Dixon, actress (*Bosom Buddies*)

July 24
Pam Tillis, country musician and daughter of Mel Tillis

July 27
Bill Engvall, comic, actor (*Blue Collar Comedy Tour*)

July 30
Bill Cartwright, center (New York Knicks, Chicago Bulls)

July 31
Dirk Blocker, actor (Lt. Jerry Bragg of *Baa Baa Black Sheep*)

August 18
Denis Leary, comic, actor
Carole Bouquet, actress (*For Your Eyes Only*)
Tan Dun, composer (*Heaven, Earth, Mankind*)

August 19
Martin Donovan, actor (*The Portrait of a Lady*)

August 21
Frank Pastore, radio personality, pitcher (Cincinnati Reds)

August 27
Bernhard Langer, PGA golfer

August 28
Rick Rossovich, actor (*Navy Seals*)

August 29
Jerry Bailey, jockey (two-time Kentucky Derby winner)

August 31
Gina Schock, drummer (The Go-Go's)

September 4
Khandi Alexander, actress (Alexx Woods of *CSI: Miami*)

September 8
Heather Thomas, actress (Jody Banks of *The Fall Guy*)

September 10
Kate Burton, actress and daughter of Richard Burton and Sybil Williams

September 11
Jeff Sluman, PGA golfer

September 12
Rachel Ward, actress (*The Thorn Birds*)

September 21
Mark Childress, novelist (*Crazy in Alabama*)

September 29
Tim Flannery, baseball player (San Diego Padres)

October 4
Bill Fagerbakke, actor (Dauber Dybinski of *Coach*)

October 6
Jonathan Alter, columnist, senior editor (*Newsweek*)

October 14
Houston Nutt, head football coach (Ole Miss Rebels)

October 17
Lawrence Bender, film/TV producer
Vincent Van Patten, actor and son of Dick Van Patten

October 24
Ron "Gardy" Gardenhire, shortstop (New York Mets) and manager (Minnesota Twins)

October 29
Dan Castellaneta, actor (voice of Homer Simpson)

October 30
Kevin Pollak, comic, actor (host of *Celebrity Poker*)

November 1
Peter Ostrum, veterinarian and child actor (Charlie Bucket of *Willy Wonka & The Chocolate Factory*)

November 6
Lori Singer, actress (*Footloose*)

November 7
Christopher Knight, actor (Peter of *The Brady Bunch*)

November 22
Donny Deutsch, TV personality (CNBC talk show host)

November 24
Denise Crosby, actress (Tasha Yar of *Star Trek*)

December 2
Randy Gardner, figure skater (five-time U.S. champion)

December 5
Art Monk, wide receiver (Washington Redskins)

December 10
Michael Clarke Duncan, actor (John Coffey of *The Green Mile*)

December 11
Peter Bagge, cartoonist (creator of comics *Hate* and *Neat Stuff*)

December 19
Kevin McHale, center (Boston Celtics)

December 22
Susan Powter, fitness expert (*Stop the Insanity!*)

December 30
Patricia Kalember, actress (Judge Taten of *Law & Order: SVU*)

Facts and Figures of 1957

President of the U.S.
Dwight D. Eisenhower
Vice President of the U.S.
Richard M. Nixon

Population of the U.S.
171,984,000

Births
4,255,000

High School Graduates
Males: 690,000
Females: 744,000

Average salary for full-time employee: $4,626
Minimum wage (per hour): $1.00
Unemployment rate: 4.3%
Rate of inflation: 3.34%

Average cost for:

Bread (lb.)	$0.19
Bacon (lb.)	$0.74
Butter (lb.)	$0.74
Eggs (doz.)	$0.57
Milk (½ gal.)	$0.50
Potatoes (10 lbs.)	$0.57
Coffee (lb.)	$1.02
Sugar (5 lbs.)	$0.55
Gasoline (gal.)	$0.24
Movie ticket	$0.50
Postage stamp	$0.03
New home	$12,220

Notable Inventions and Firsts

January 5: The Dodgers' baseball great Jackie Robinson retires rather than be traded to the New York Giants.

January 6: CBS network censors insist that singer Elvis Presley be shown only from the waist up for his third appearance on *The Ed Sullivan Show*.

June 2: Soviet First Secretary Khrushchev appears on the CBS program, *Face the Nation*, marking the first American television appearance by a Soviet leader since World War II.

July 29: The International Atomic Energy Agency is established by the United Nations to promote peaceful uses of nuclear energy.

August 28–29: United States Senator Strom Thurmond of South Carolina filibusters for a record 24 hours and 19 minutes in opposition to the Civil Rights Act of 1957.

October 24: French fashion pioneer Christian Dior dies in Italy at age 52, leaving his assistant, Yves Saint Laurent, to take over leadership of the Dior fashion house.

1957: Engineers Alfred Fielding and Marc Chavannes accidentally invent bubble wrap while trying to create plastic wallpaper.

1957: The first issue of *Gentleman's Quarterly*, or *GQ*, is published.

1957: For the first time United States history, approximately as many women as men are registered to vote in the United States.

1957 Quiz Answers

1. *Gunsmoke*, page 24
2. Peddle pushers, page 13
3. Althea Gibson, page 60
4. 10th anniversary, page 6
5. Mackinac Bridge, page 74
6. Theodor Seuss Geisel, page 46
7. Milwaukee Braves, page 65
8. Alec Guinness, page 39

Sports Winners

NFL: Detroit Lions defeat Cleveland Browns
World Series: Milwaukee Braves defeat New York Yankees
Stanley Cup: Montreal Canadiens defeat Boston Bruins
The Masters: Doug Ford
PGA Championship: Lionel Hebert
NBA: Boston Celtics defeat St. Louis Hawks

Live It Again 1957

PROJECT EDITOR	Barb Sprunger
CREATIVE DIRECTOR	Brad Snow
COPYWRITER & RESEARCH ASSISTANT	Becky Sarasin
EDITORIAL ASSISTANT	Laurie Lehman
COPY SUPERVISOR	Deborah Morgan
PRODUCTION ARTIST SUPERVISOR	Erin Brandt
PRODUCTION ARTIST	Edith Teegarden
COPY EDITORS	Mary O'Donnell, Sam Schneider
PHOTOGRAPHY SUPERVISOR	Tammy Christian
NOSTALGIA EDITOR	Ken Tate
PUBLISHING SERVICES DIRECTOR	Brenda Gallmeyer

Printed in China
First Printing: 2012
Library of Congress Control Number: 2011942613

Customer Service
LiveItAgain.com
(800) 829-5865

We would like to thank Curtis Publishing for the art prints used in this book. For fine-art prints and more information on the artists featured in *Live It Again 1957* contact Curtis Publishing, Indianapolis, IN 46202, (317) 633-2070, All rights reserved, www.curtispublishing.com

We would like to thank the Wisconsin Historical Society for the use of their online Photograph and Image collection (www.wisconsinhistory.org) and CNH America LLC.

1 2 3 4 5 6 7 8 9